Decorating

TRICKS OF
THE TRADE

Decorating

Bob Tattersall

Pelham Books

First published in Great Britain by
PELHAM BOOKS LTD
44 Bedford Square
London WC1
1978

ISBN 0 7207 1036 7

Printed and bound in Hong Kong.

To Diana,
With whom I have happily
decorated our home

Contents

List of Line Illustrations   9

Introduction   11

1   Preparation   12

2   Paints and Painting   34

3   Wallpapers   73

Postscript   121

Index   123

Line
Illustrations

		page
Fig. 1	Support for a scaffold board	16
Fig. 2	Scrapers	17
Fig. 3	Shave hooks	18
Fig. 4	Using a blowlamp	24
Fig. 5	A hawk	28
Fig. 6	Filling cracks	29
Fig. 7	How to hold a putty knife	30
Fig. 8	Filling large holes	31
Fig. 9	Types of brush	39
Fig. 10	How to hold a varnish brush	44
Fig. 11	How to hold a wall brush	44
Fig. 12	Holding a paint kettle	55
Fig. 13	Painting large surfaces	58
Fig. 14	Order of painting a door	61
Fig. 15	Cutting in	63
Fig. 16	Filling a roller with paint	69
Fig. 17	Wallpapering: order of work	85
Fig. 18.	Pasting the paper	91
Fig. 19	Papering: the end of the wall	97
Fig. 20	Papering round light switches	99
Fig. 21	Papering round a door	101
Fig. 22	Papering round a window	103
Fig. 23	Folding paper for the ceiling	116

Introduction

Never before was life so easy for the do-it-yourself decorator. In the past few years whole new ranges of products have been introduced that not only look better and last longer, but also are easier to apply. Now it is really possible for you to achieve a professional finish. Yet as you go about decorating your home you will probably realize that there is one way in which these new products can't help you – they won't tell you all those wrinkles and dodges that the professional decorator has learned from experience, that enable him to do a better job more quickly.

It is the aim of this book, the first of a series, to let you in on those secrets. As you read through these instructions on home decorating you will, every so often, come across a paragraph picked out with the symbol ➔ and set in bold type. You will know then that you are reading a trick of the trade.

1 Preparation

Before you can begin even to think of applying paint and paper, you must get the surfaces ready to receive them. This preparation is the most tiresome and tiring part of any decoration job, and since at this stage you are not producing anything beautiful, the work seems to lack incentive. But you ignore this preparation at your peril. For although decorating materials are nowadays much tougher, longer lasting and easier to apply than they have ever been, you will not get satisfactory results if you do not put them on a suitably prepared surface.

In any event it is in the preparation that the do-it-yourselfer can really score over the tradesman. For preparation takes time – and time is something the professional cannot spare. Although he knows all about the necessary preparation, he has to get the job done quickly in order to keep the price down to a competitive level, and so here and there he has to skimp a bit.

Put simply, the preparation consists of ensuring that the surfaces you are going to decorate will be stable, clean, dry and suitably primed for the decorative finish. You start with the walls and ceiling. If you are working in a room that has previously been papered, then this paper will have to be stripped off. Many do-it-yourselfers wonder whether this is strictly necessary – after all, they say, there can be nothing wrong with two layers of paper because in many instances wallpaper goes on top of lining paper. But if you do put new paper on top of old you are taking a risk. You might get away with it, and you might not. For the paste under the old paper will have become brittle with age, and will therefore have lost its strength.

When the paste of the new paper goes on the wall, its moisture can get through to the old, and loosen it. As a result, in no time at all both lots of paper may be peeling away from the wall. That is why most professionals prefer to strip off the old paper.

If the walls and/or ceiling have been treated with emulsion paint, they must be given a thorough wash down and rinsing to get rid of the accumulation of grease and grime.

With the plaster thus treated, examine it for any defects such as holes and cracks, or loose and crumbling patches, and make these good.

Then you can turn to the woodwork. If this is in pretty good condition, and you are doing a repaint merely to freshen it up, or for a change of colour, then all you need do with it is wash and rinse it, then give it a rub down with abrasive paper, and you are ready to paint. If there are a few more defects than that – perhaps a few scuffs and knocks, with the odd bit of paint surface chipped off here and there – then wash down and rinse, trying not to soak any bare areas of wood. Then be a bit more thorough with your rubbing down, and fill up any holes and cracks. Use a fine-surface filler to bring the areas of chipped paint up to the level of the rest. However, where the paintwork is in really bad condition – cracked and flaking, blisters here and there – it must be stripped off completely, back to the bare wood. Metalwork, if there is any in your room, is treated in a similar way.

Now I will tell you how to carry out these various operations.

First Clear the Room

The do-it-yourselfer, trying to cause as little domestic disturbance as possible, often allows the family to go on using the room he or she is about to decorate, and tries to work round them. That is a big mistake. You will not get

13

such a good result, and you will not finish so quickly. In fact, in the long run you might even cause more upheaval.

Clear the decks completely before you begin. If you can take all the furniture out into another room, then do so. Otherwise, arrange it all together in the centre of the room, and throw dust sheets over it. But leave enough room to place access equipment over or round it. For dust sheets you can use old bed-sheets or buy polythene dust sheets, which are not all that expensive. Pictures and ornaments must be taken down and stored out of harm's way. The curtains, too, must be unhooked – it's a good opportunity to have them cleaned or washed – and the curtain track unscrewed, so that you will be able to deal properly with the window frames. Lampshades need to be temporarily removed.

You don't want dust flying around in a room in which you are painting – it will spoil the finish if it gets on to wet paint – so as part of your preparation you should dust all surfaces, and vacuum clean everywhere.

Ideally, too, you ought to take up your floor coverings, and if they are loose that should not be a problem. However, if you have fitted carpets, that might involve you in unwanted expense: most carpets need to be professionally stretched when laid, to avoid uneven wear, which means that you would have to call in a carpet fitter (and pay him) to put the carpet back when you have finished. But here's a dodge. **Place dust sheets on the floor – which you ought to do whether you have a fitted carpet or not – and to make sure that they will stay in place, leaving no gaps through which paint or wallpaper paste could seep through and stain your carpet, fasten them all round the edges with masking tape. Position this masking tape carefully round the edges of the room, so that it just covers the edge of the carpet, but allows you to work on the skirting board. When the job is finished, you will be able to peel off the tape without harming the carpet.**

14

Reaching High Places

You cannot decorate a room and stand on the floor the whole time, because you would not be able to reach the ceiling and the higher parts of the wall and woodwork. You must have some means of access at all stages during decorating.

I want to stress how important it is that you have proper and safe means of reaching high places. **Many amateur decorators think that all you need is an ordinary pair of household steps, but for many operations that simply will not do. The area you can reach while standing on steps is very limited, and it is such a nuisance continually getting down to move them that you will be tempted to stretch just that little bit farther, which is tiring and sometimes dangerous. Certainly the professional would not risk injury in that way, nor would he tire himself out needlessly. He uses a scaffold board.**

A Home-made Scaffold Board

Go along to your local timber yard and buy some unplaned timber at least 230 mm (9 ins) wide and 38 mm ($1\frac{1}{2}$ ins) thick and long enough to suit the size of your room. Professional scaffold boards are shaped at the ends and strengthened with metal strips. But you don't need to worry about this – it is merely to stop the board from being damaged because it will be subjected to rougher treatment than your home-made one.

The professional usually suspends his board between two pairs of steps. You will probably have only one pair. Perhaps you can borrow an additional pair from a neighbour. Otherwise, you will have to improvize, by using a packing case, small chest, stout stool – anything strong enough to take your weight. Do, however, be sure that everything is stable before you risk clambering up on it because you can have a very nasty fall indeed if your

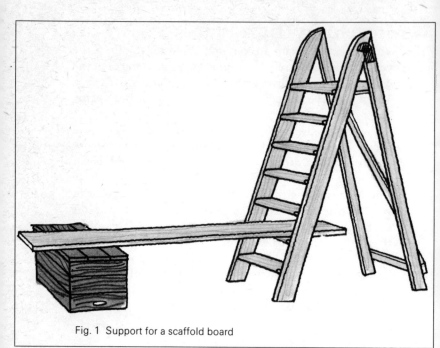

Fig. 1 Support for a scaffold board

scaffolding arrangement is rickety.

In my own case, a pair of large, five-tread steps does very well for all manner of jobs around the house, and that I regard as part of my home maintenance kit. Then we also have a pair of small two-tread steps that are light enough for my wife to carry around the house when she wants steps with which to reach the tops of wardrobes or kitchen cupboards. I borrow these and use them in conjunction with my own to support my scaffold board.

Such simple scaffolding arrangements are quite suitable for most rooms in the house. However, when you come to tackle the hall and landing, a more complicated set-up will be called for, depending on the shape of the area in question.

16

Scraping Tools

To tackle your first job – stripping off wallpaper – you will need a scraper, and other scrapers will be called for when you come to deal with the paintwork. So let us look at the kit of scrapers you require.

Scrapers

Scrapers look exactly like the filling knives you use for stopping up holes, but they are in fact totally different tools, and not interchangeable: for a scraper to work properly it must have a rigid blade, whereas the blade of the filling knife must be flexible. So you need a set of each.

·Scrapers come in a range of sizes. For stripping off ← wallpaper, the professional would probably use one with a 100-mm (4-in.) blade. You, however, might

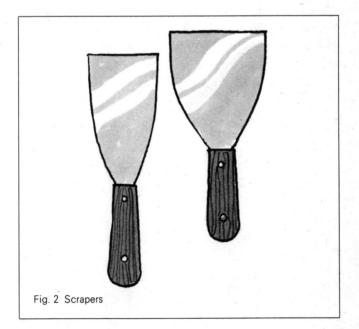

Fig. 2 Scrapers

find that too unwieldy, and prefer to settle for a 75-mm (3-in.) blade. Again, the 75-mm blade would be too big on paintwork, because the wood is not perfectly flat, and here you should go for a 50-mm (2-in.) blade.

Scrapers with a 25-mm (1-in.) wide blade are available, but the professional tends to regard these as paint spats – ie for mixing and stirring paint. Purpose-made paint spats are also on sale.

It is easy to recognize a good-quality scraper, for it will be what is known as 'tanged' – ie its blade will run right through the handle, which will consist of two halves, one each side of the metal. Whether you go to the expense of buying top-quality tools will depend on how much you think you will use them.

Shave Hooks

For scraping off on narrow strips, the professional would tend to use a shave hook. Basically, there are three types of shave hook: the triangular one for flat surfaces, the

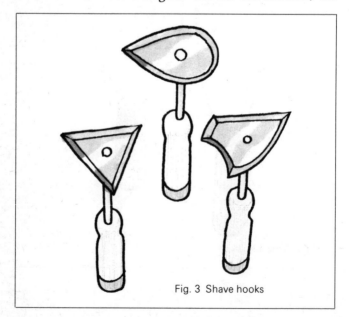

Fig. 3 Shave hooks

heart-shaped one for curved mouldings, and the combination hook, so called because it combines the shapes of the other two. You ought really to have both a triangular and heart-shaped hook, but you will probably want to buy only one, so settle for the combination tool.

To use a scraper, you place the blade on the surface and push it upwards, or away from you on a horizontal surface. But to use a shave hook you pull downwards, or towards you. You can use much stronger pressure with a shave hook. That is why the decorator prefers them when he is burning off window frames, for since the paintwork does not have to be so soft he need not keep the blowlamp's flame playing on it for so long, and thus there is less risk of his overheating the glass, and cracking it.

Stripping Off Wallpaper

To strip off wallpaper, you need a bucket, a large – 100- or 125-mm (4- or 5-in.) brush – and the 75-mm (3-in.) scraper already discussed.

Pour some water into your bucket, then brush it on to the walls, taking care that you do not get any on the floor, especially upstairs, where it might seep down to the room below. The water gets through to the glue behind and breaks down the old paste. **You can get stripping powders to add to the water: they make the water cling more readily to the surface, and not run off down the wall uselessly. The professional, however, tends not to use them, although many squeeze a few drops of washing-up liquid into their stripping water, since this seems to have the same effect.**

Work on one wall at a time, or on the ceiling (with which you should begin if it is papered). Soak it thoroughly once, then go over it again, giving it another dousing. The important thing is that you must let the water do the work. If you try to remove the paper too soon, before the water has completely broken down the old glue, you will find yourself wielding your scraper too vigorously, and will dig into the plaster below, gouging out holes that you will then have to fill. Paper that is ready to come off should peel away from the wall readily in long strips.

When all the paper is off, go over the wall again with water and the scraper, getting rid of any old lumps of paste and paper. Then you can move on to the next wall.

Washable and Painted-over Papers

If it's a washable paper you are trying to remove, then you will straightaway come across a snag. Washable paper, as you might expect, has an impermeable surface, and water will be unable to get through to the paste behind. **The way out is to score the surface in some way, to make holes through which the water can pass. You can make holes with a scraper or a wire brush, but in both cases there is a risk that you will scratch the plaster underneath, and you might be better off using coarse glasspaper.** Papers that have been painted over present a problem similar to that posed by washables, and should be treated in the same way.

Anaglyptas

If it's a relief decoration such as Anaglypta that you are dealing with, you should use a sharp-pointed putty knife (see page 27), held with the flat of the blade at an acute angle to the wall, to dig into the material and strip off the top layer of paper. The bottom one can then be treated just like ordinary wallpaper. A Supaglypta (these different kinds of paper are all described on page 71) would be more difficult to deal with, however, and you would do better to rake its surface with a wire brush.

Vinyls

Easiest of all papers to strip are vinyls, for they consist of a top layer of plastic bonded to paper underneath. Take hold of one corner of the plastic surface, and peel it away in one length. If you begin at the bottom of the wall you don't even need to climb a pair of steps, for you can strip off the whole length while standing on the floor. The backing paper then stays on the wall to act as a lining, and the new surface goes directly on top of it. When you have decorated the room a couple of times with a vinyl, however, and you have two layers of backing paper left on, then the time has come to strip them off. You do so just as though they were ordinary wallpapers.

Washing Down

Walls and ceilings that have been painted must be washed down. Even if your paintwork needs no other preparation, it will require this to get rid of all dirt and grease.

When washing down, against all common sense ◄─── you begin at the bottom of the wall and work upwards. And that means that you tackle the ceiling last. The reason for this is that if you worked the other way about, the dirt you loosened would cause a build-up of grime lower down the wall that would be very difficult to remove.

To wash down, you need a bucket, plus a rag or sponge and (preferably) decorator's detergent. You can get by with ordinary household detergent, but the proper stuff is stronger and coarser, and will slightly roughen the surface, as well as getting rid of grease, thus keying it to receive the later finishes.

Mix the detergent with water according to the instructions, soak your rag in it, then wring it out. Rub it over the surface in a circular motion to loosen the dirt. Rinse out your rag in the detergent, and with top-to-bottom vertical strokes get rid of the loosened dirt. If the walls are very grimy, you might have to repeat this operation two or three times. When you seem to have removed all the dirt, move along and tackle a similar patch next to it, and go on in this way until you have completed a whole band along the bottom of the wall. Next tackle another band on top of it, and finally one on top of that – the walls in most rooms will split conveniently into three horizontal bands.

When you have completed the top band, rinse the whole wall immediately with clean water before going on to another wall. When rinsing, you do work from the top downwards. Use plenty of water, changing it frequently.

If there is any mould growth on the walls, wash down with a solution of 1 part of ordinary domestic bleach to 16 of water. Leave for about two hours, then wash down with detergent, finally rinsing off with the bleach solution once more.

You must let the paintwork dry out thoroughly before you apply paint or wallpaper to it.

Stripping Off Paint

There are two ways in which you can strip paint off woodwork: with a blowlamp or with a chemical stripper. The professional unquestionably prefers the former, for it is quicker and cheaper.

Blowlamps

At one time I would have hesitated to recommend a blowlamp to the do-it-yourselfer, for the old-fashioned petrol- and paraffin-operated lamps were tricky to use and potentially dangerous. However, most blowlamps now work off liquid gas, which is a safe and highly convenient fuel.

The professional with a gas lamp will probably have a large cylinder like the ones that power cooking stoves in caravans, and his lamp will be connected to this by a long, thin hose. He will have different nozzles to fit to the lamp to give a flame suitable for large or small areas of paintwork.

The advantages of this type of blowlamp over the

small type with gas cylinder attached are that gas is cheaper when bought in large cylinders and does not run out so often, thus sparing you the bother of frequently shopping for replacement cylinders; and as you move your hand up and down the work you are holding just a light blowlamp head, and not a canister of gas as well, which no matter how small can become quite tiring at the end of a long day's work.

If you are a camper or own a caravan, then you should buy the larger type of blowlamp. You buy the blowlamp and hose as a separate item, and connect it up to the gas cylinder you already have for your cooker. Otherwise, unless you plan to do a lot of burning off, you will probably want to settle for one of the portable lamps with its own canister of gas.

Although gas-operated lamps are not dangerous, there is one safety point you should observe. When you screw on a new canister, there is bound to be a slight escape of gas when the cylinder is first punctured. So this operation is best done out of doors, or at least well away from a naked flame.

When you are burning off, your aim should be to scorch the timber as little as possible. And remember that old decorator's saying – the flame can only scorch bare wood, not wood that is protected by paint. So start burning off by tackling any small, fiddly bits such as the moulding on a panelled door. If you left these until last, the flame would be playing on nearby bare wood, and would scorch it.

First, let your blowlamp flame play on the paintwork to warm it. Hold the lamp in one hand and your scraper in the other. Then go over it again, this time scraping off. **On large areas and vertical strips, the scraper should always be below the flame; on horizontal ones it should follow behind it. That way you will not get burned. Always keep the scraper at an angle – ie its scraping edge not horizontal – so that your hand will**

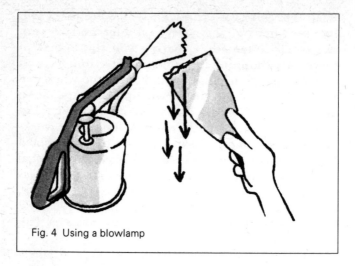

Fig. 4 Using a blowlamp

not be directly under hot paint as it drops to the floor, and if the scraper slips forward into the path of the lamp, your hand will not move into the flame.

The paint that drops off will be hot and can burn. If you want to protect the floor covering, put down a sheet of hardboard. Don't, of course, use any combustible material.

If you are working in an old house with many coats of old paint you will probably find that your scrapers get clogged very quickly. Before you start to burn off, make up a strong solution of garden lime in water and brush it on the paint. That will stop the clogging.

The competent professional uses a blowlamp even on window frames, although if you have tried this you will probably know how easy it is to crack the glass with the heat of the flame. How does he avoid this? He turns the flame down low, keeps it continually on the move, and he uses a shave hook (see section on scrapers) for removing the paint. He is particularly careful in the corners of the frame, where there is often a large build-up of paint, not to leave the flame playing on one spot for too long.

Strippers

If, even with this advice, you find that you are breaking the glass, change over to a chemical paint stripper. It is as well to use these on metal, too, which can be distorted by heat.

The mistake many do-it-yourselfers make with ⬅ **chemical strippers is that they do not allow the strippers enough time to do their work. They want to start scraping almost the instant they have brushed on the stripper. In fact, you have to leave it there for some time – follow the manufacturer's instructions – before you can begin to remove the paint.** I find it a good idea to brush on one application, leave it for about ten minutes, then brush on more stripper and leave this for the same time. The first application causes an initial bubbling up of the paint, and the second will then stay in place and be less liable to run down the surface while getting at the layers of paint underneath.

If you have to remove any emulsion paint from a ⬅ **plaster wall, because it is flaking, then this can usually be done very easily with a scraper. With stubborn bits, use a diluted chemical stripper – three parts of stripper to one part of water.**

A chemical stripper needs to be neutralized when you have finished, otherwise it might affect the new paint you put on. Usually you neutralize with either water or white spirit – follow the manufacturer's instructions. As a general guide, though, you can use water on indoor woodwork, but white spirit is better out of doors because there is more risk of water introducing damp into exterior woodwork.

There are safety precautions to observe, too, when you are using a chemical stripper. Always wear rubber gloves because these materials are caustic and you might burn your hands. You should avoid inhaling their fumes, so always make sure that the room in which you are working is well ventilated. In particular don't smoke; not because of the fire hazard, but because you inhale much more strongly when smoking and there is a greater risk of your drawing in the fumes.

Whatever method of stripping you use, when you have finished you should give the timber a thorough sanding to get rid of any small flecks of paint still left, and generally smooth down the work.

Getting Rid of Whitewash

Whitewash and non-washable distempers have not been used for years, but you still come across them when renovating old houses. You cannot put paint on top of them, and they have to be removed. **For this you need plenty of water, and an old short-haired brush or rag. Dip the brush or rag into the water, and attack the surface vigorously with a circular motion, working the whitewash up into a scum. Then rinse it off with a rag and lots of clean water.**

This is a very unpleasant job, especially as whitewash was so often put on ceilings, but it has to be done.

If you are in any doubt as to whether a surface is whitewashed or not, try washing it. Whitewash will come off; emulsion paint (and washable distemper, which can be treated like emulsion paint) will stay in place.

Rubbing Down Paintwork

Large, flat areas of paintwork, such as a flush door, should always be rubbed down before you paint them. Even if the existing coat was superbly applied and is still in good condition, there will at the very least be a few specks of dust that settled on the old paint before it dried out. And, of course, you may well find imperfections in the paintwork – the odd run here and there, for instance.

The best material to use for rubbing down

paintwork (as opposed to bare surfaces) is wet-and-dry, which as its name implies is an abrasive paper that you can use wet or dry. It is far better to use it wet, however. You dunk it in a bucket of water, then use it to rub down the surface. Rub round in all directions, and not just in one straight line, otherwise you might wear out a groove in the surface. One of the many advantages of wet-and-dry is that, when used wet, it does not cause dust. This is especially important when you are dealing with very old paint which might contain lead (modern paints are non-toxic). If you rub down with ordinary glasspaper you will raise a dust that contains lead, which you could breathe with possible harmful results.

Wet-and-dry is an expensive material, and you can ◄ make it last longer if you smear it with ordinary household soap first – it will still do its job. When you have finished rubbing down with wet-and-dry, rinse the surface well with clean water and a sponge. Then leather off with a wash leather. Any paintwork that survives this treatment you will know to be perfectly sound and fully able to receive subsequent coats of paint without the need for stripping.

Filling the Cracks

When all the surfaces have been stripped and/or rubbed down, you can tackle the filling. Incidentally, when should you fill? Before or after you have put on the priming coat? The professionals disagree on that point. Some have told me that you should apply the primer first, because it will impart a coating to which the filler can stick; others say that the priming coat should go on last because the filler needs priming like any other bare surface. So it seems that the choice is up to you. But I like the advice of one old, very experienced professional who said that he would always prime before filling exterior woodwork, but fill first indoors.

Small holes and cracks are best stopped up with a cellulose filler and there are two tools you use for applying this – the filling knife and the putty knife. The filling knife is usually used on cracks, especially long ones, in the middle of a flat surface. As explained on page 15, a filling knife looks just like a scraper, but has a flexible blade.

You also need a container for your filling material. Do-it-yourselfers tend to make do with an old plate or saucer, but this is inadequate if you have a big job that will require a lot of filler. Professionals use what they call a

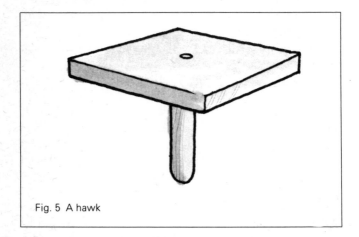

Fig. 5 A hawk

hawk, and it is very easy for you to improvize one. Take a small sheet of plywood, about 300 mm (12 ins) square, and in the middle and at right angles to the board, screw or nail a short length of wood as a handle. And there's your hawk.

If it is a long, thin crack you are dealing with, begin by raking it along its length with the pointed edge of the knife. The idea of this is to enlarge the crack enough to take the filler, and to get rid of any loose material. Load your knife with filler, then draw it across the crack at right angles to its length, flexing the blade as you do so, to push the filler well in. Then draw the knife down the length of the crack, with the blade flat on the surface, to remove any surplus filler.

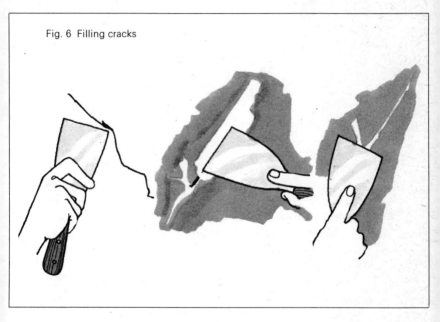

Fig. 6 Filling cracks

The putty knife (sometimes called the clypt putty knife) is spear-shaped, and is the tool with which a glazier applies putty when fixing a pane of glass in a window. The decorator uses it, however, to fill small holes. You hold the handle in the palm of your hand, and extend your forefinger along the blade to steady it. The straight edge of the blade is used to apply the filler, and the curved one to remove any surplus. The straight edge of the putty knife blade is very useful, too, for applying filler in an angle – eg between a door frame and the wall.

29

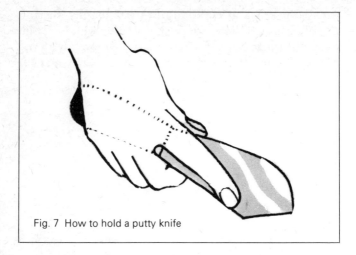

Fig. 7 How to hold a putty knife

Whatever type of hole or crack you are filling, try to leave the filler slightly proud of the surface. Then when it has dried you can rub it over with glasspaper to sand it down flush.

If you have extensive areas of bad wall surface – large holes or big stretches of crumbling plaster – then cellulose filler will be too expensive, and you should use plaster instead. This is available in small packs.

Hack away, with a trowel or scraper, at the defective area until you have got rid of all the loose and crumbling plaster, and you come to what is called a firm edge. If the base coat of the plaster, which may also be plaster, but could be sand and cement rendering, is suspect, hack this off as well until the wall behind is exposed. On lath and plaster walls it does not matter if you have to expose the wall back to the laths.

Apply the plaster to the wall using either a trowel or a filling knife – even a float trowel where the hole is big enough – putting on enough to allow it to stand slightly proud of the surrounding wall. Then go over with a short length of timber that is straight and true, to remove

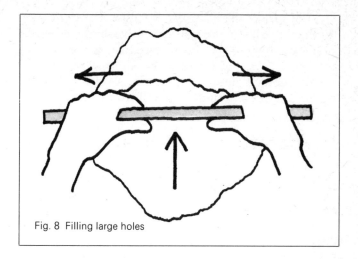

Fig. 8 Filling large holes

surplus plaster, and finish the repair flush with the surface. Lightly stroke the new plaster with a trowel or knife moistened in water to make the surface smooth. Finally, feather out the edges with a damp sponge, and the repair will be hardly detectable. Then leave it to dry out thoroughly.

If the hole or crack is a deep one, it should be filled ◄── in two operations. The surface of the first application of filler should be scratched with the trowel or knife, to key it, then allowed to dry, after which the top coat can be added.

A wall that you intend to paint needs much more attention from the filling point of view than one that will be covered with paper, for a paper can hide cracks that will show through the paint. **In fact, if your wall is ◄── covered in small cracks it will be a never-ending job trying to fill them, and a better treatment would be lining paper, followed by thick wallpaper. If you insist on a painted finish, then you should apply a lining paper suitable for receiving paint. More information on this subject will be found on page 110.**

A fine surface filler is available for use where you want to ensure a really superb painted finish, which will usually be on woodwork. The fine surface filler is not for deep holes or cracks, but for covering up small defects and imperfections. You apply it with a broad filling knife, which you flex as you draw the filler across the surface, spreading it well out.

Preparation for Metalwork

Metal is treated pretty much like woodwork, but there are two big differences. For a start, you cannot use a blowlamp on metal because the heat will damage it. So if any paint needs to be stripped from metal you must scrape it off or use a chemical stripper. Fortunately, paint does not cling so well to metal as to wood, so this does not pose too much of a problem. The other difference is that ferrous metals produce something that is a big enemy of paint – rust. If you apply paint on top of rust, it will lift off in no time.

Fortunately, almost the only place where you will find metal inside the average British home is in the window frames, and most of those installed since the war have been treated during manufacture to make them rust-resistant. However, when metal window frames were first introduced during the 1930s they were not made rust-resistant, and most of these are now suffering from some degree of attack by rust. In a few cases, the attacks are so bad that the frames are by now seriously pitted – especially those that have not been well cared for over the years – and in some instances rust has caused the frames to warp so that the windows will not open and close properly. When things get as serious as this, the only answer is to have the old frames replaced with new ones.

If the attack is not too bad, you can try scraping the rust off – a wire brush in an electric drill is a good tool, but wear goggles to protect your eyes.

Some of these old frames, of course, have been so well

cared for that they are in perfect condition. These and the post-war ones are treated as though they were wood. If the paint on them is in good condition, just wash it down, but if it is defective it will have to be stripped. Take care when scraping that you do not dig too deeply into any protective coat of galvanizing, and that you do not leave the bare surfaces wet for this would cause rust.

In an old house you might come across iron and steel in other parts of your room. The fireplace could be made of iron, for instance, or you could find the odd bracket or similar fixture. Fortunately these will not be so exposed to moisture as window frames, so rust should not be as much of a problem. But any rust will have to be got rid of – use a wire brush or emery cloth, depending on the nature of the surface and how bad the pitting is.

Other metals you might find in your home are aluminium and copper – the former on window frames, especially if you have had double glazing installed recently, and the latter on pipes for domestic water and central heating.

Aluminium has a smooth and rather greasy surface. If you want to paint it, wash it down with white spirit and, while it is still wet, rub it with wet-and-dry abrasive paper. Clean off with a clean rag soaked in white spirit, and then wipe it down with a clean dry cloth. Prime it (see page 52) without delay.

Copper is a metal that does not take paint well, and as a result is best left unpainted, though if you want to hide ugly old pipes treat them as described for aluminium. But when you rub down make sure no particles of copper that fall off are left on adjacent areas, for when you paint these later green copper stains could show through.

2 Paints and Painting

Paint is the most versatile and the most popular decorating material available today. You can get a paint to cover just about every material you are likely to meet in the modern home, indoors or out. And not only will the paint look attractive but it will offer maximum protection to your home. Furthermore, paints are easily the cheapest form of decorating you can choose. And many people would tell you that they also are just about the easiest decorative material to apply.

Certainly, enormous strides have been made in paint technology in recent years, advances which have made paints not only longer lasting and better to look at, but also easier for the decorator to handle. Let's take a closer look at paints and painting.

First Choose Your Finish

Before you can start to paint, you have to decide what type of finish you want for the various surfaces in your home. A bewildering array of new paints has been introduced in recent years. The manufacturers have strained to steal a march on each other by introducing products that they claim to be one step ahead of the competition. As a result, you can be forgiven for thinking that you need to be an industrial chemist to enter a decorator's shop these days. But in fact things are not as confusing as they have been made to seem, so here's a quick guide to what's what on the paint shelf. Incidentally, all paints made by a reputable manufacturer are durable and easily washed.

Oil Paints – Gloss

For the maximum protection of woodwork and metal you should use an oil paint, which comes in two types – the liquid form, and the thixotropic (sometimes known as a gel or non-drip). A liquid gloss gives the best, toughest and longest lasting finish of any type of paint. It is, however, the trickiest paint of all to apply, because you have to judge exactly how much to put on the surface – too little, and you don't get a sufficiently protective film; too much and it tends to run. (See pages 57–60 for exactly how to apply these paints.) Brushes used for liquid gloss are the most difficult to clean, because generally you must use a proper solvent – paraffin, white spirit (often called turps substitute) or a proprietary brush cleaner. (Full details of how to clean your brush are given on page 71.)

Many manufacturers tend to think of their range as being in two main streams – trade and DIY – and their basis for the distinction is simple: if the paint is liquid it's for the trade; if it's a thixotropic it's for the consumer. In a way they are right, because gel paints are much easier to apply and many of them come with a special additive that enables you to clean the brush afterwards in a solution of water and detergent. Easy brush cleaning, of course, is a big plus for the amateur decorator, but the professional, having been trained from his apprentice days to clean his brushes properly, is not so dismayed by this task.

However, professionals often use a gel paint when they want to do a quick job, because a gel can be applied more thickly, so you can get away with fewer coats. On the other hand, gel glosses tend to be more expensive.

Oil Paints – Eggshell

Eggshell paints are oil paints without a shiny surface. They have now diminished in popularity because of competition from the newer types of paint. I will describe these new types later, but a lot of professional decorators like the eggshell paints.

Emulsion Paints

Plaster surfaces do not need the same protection as wood and metal, and they have more imperfections which would tend to be highlighted by the sheen of a gloss. So on these you can use an emulsion, which is cheaper, easier to apply, quick drying, does not have the same lingering smell, and you clean your brush afterwards in water.

Emulsions, too, come in liquid and gel form. Once again, the manufacturers tend to think of the liquid variety as a trade product because it is slightly more difficult to apply, and the gel as being for do-it-yourselfers. And once again, they are not entirely correct, for, as with gloss paints, a gel emulsion can be applied more thickly, and therefore requires fewer coats – a fact by no means entirely without appeal to the tradesman.

Although I have said that emulsion paints do not offer the same protection as gloss, they are nevertheless very tough, and the modern ones made by reputable manufacturers are fully able to stand up to any conditions they will meet in the home, even in the areas of the hardest wear, such as kitchens and bathrooms.

Gloss Emulsion

There is also an in-between paint known as gloss emulsion, which combines the advantages of both types of paint. Just like an emulsion paint, it is easy to apply, there is no lingering smell, it dries quickly, and you wash your brushes out in water afterwards. Yet it does have a shiny surface, and you can apply it as a top coat on wood and metal, as well as using it on walls. So it is a highly versatile product. However, it is not so tough or shiny as the true gloss, and many brands of this type of paint cannot be used out of doors. The trade tends to regard it as a convenience product for the not-so-skilled amateur.

Silk Finish Emulsion

Many emulsions have a silk finish, which represents quite an advance in paint technology. Achieving the finish was not the problem; the trouble was that at one time silk finishes tended to go shiny when you washed them. However, that has been overcome, and emulsions with a silky sheen are now among the most popular paints on the market, and some manufacturers recommend them for woodwork, too.

Silk Finish Gloss

Finally, of recent years, a series of paints that are glosses, with a silky finish has been introduced. These are – to date – the ultimate in convenience, for they are all-surface paints (you can use them on walls and woodwork in any part of the house), thixotropic, almost as easy to apply as emulsions, and it is easy to clean your brushes afterwards. However, they are expensive to buy.

Your Kit of Brushes

In just about every book on home decorating that I have seen I have come across the advice that you should buy the best paintbrushes you can afford. I am not so sure that this is good advice. Certainly it is what the professional does, but he is using his brushes every day of his working life, and they have to stand up to an immense amount of wear. It could be that if you bought a brush of the same quality you would have to throw it away long before it had worn out because you had neglected to clean it properly after use, or it had got lost, or even damaged in some way. But there is another point. **The professional buys an expensive brush because its bristles are long and full, and will hold more paint. As a result he does not have to keep charging his brush so often, and can spend more of his time actually using the brush to put paint on the surface, rather than dipping it into a paint pot.** The snag about this from the amateur's point of view is that a fully loaded brush, particularly a large one, is very heavy, and might put a heavy strain on your wrist. You would get tired quickly, and would get a poorer finish with it than with a less expensive brush.

Now don't get me wrong. I am not suggesting that you buy really cheap brushes. Far from it. A bad brush is a waste of time. The paint will not flow from it properly, and it keeps shedding its hairs as you work. You are wasting your time and money in buying such equipment. But there is no need to go to the other extreme and buy top-quality tradesmen's tools. If you shop for your paintbrushes at an ordinary do-it-yourself shop, by all means get the best they have on offer. But if you go to a builder's merchant, or some other place where the tradesman buys his equipment, beware of paying out for something with a quality beyond your needs and a price beyond your pocket.

Anyway, let us now take a closer look at paintbrushes.

The best material to use for the hairs of a paintbrush is bristle, which grows on the wild pig. Paintbrush bristles are now imported from Asia – China, and, to a lesser extent, India – and they are becoming increasingly rare. Because of this, on some of the large brushes, and the cheaper ones, substitute materials such as horsehair and vegetable fibre are being used. They do not make such a good-quality brush.

Wall and Ceiling Brushes

Just as there are two basic types of paint, so there are two distinct types of brush. One is for applying gloss paint to the woodwork of your home, the other for use with water-based paints (emulsions). The latter brush is known as a wall brush. You can buy wall brushes in 100-, 125- and 150-mm (4-, 5- and 6-in.) sizes. The remarks I made earlier about paint-holding capacity apply very strongly here. The bigger the brush, the less time you have to spend recharging it, but it will be heavier and consequently more tiring to wield. A fully loaded 150-mm brush would, I think, be very hard on the wrist of an untrained amateur, but with a little practice you should be able to cope with a 125-mm one, which would be more satisfactory than a 100-mm brush.

The wall brush has a big brother, known as the distemper brush. This is used for ceiling work, and it gets its name because at one time distemper was commonly used on the ceilings of our homes. The distemper brush is

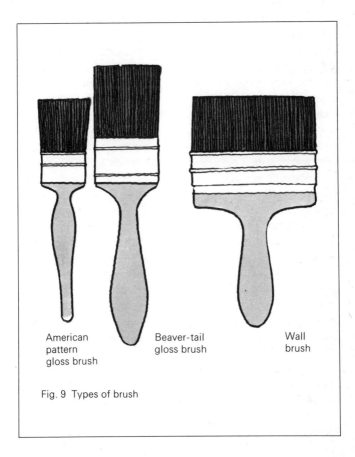

American
pattern
gloss brush

Beaver-tail
gloss brush

Wall
brush

Fig. 9 Types of brush

175 mm (7 ins) wide, and is extremely heavy when fully charged with paint. However, the professional finds it less tiring to use such a brush than to be continually stooping down – with a consequent strain on the back – to re-load a smaller brush with paint. I don't think that you would agree with this, however, and so I would advise you when painting a ceiling to use a wall brush, and as big a one as you can cope with comfortably.

How do you recognize whether a wall brush is any good or not? The best-quality wall brushes are of pure bristle, the visible length of which is about 100 mm (4 ins). The metal band holding the bristles in place will be copper – you must have non-rusting metal, because these brushes are continually in contact with a paint that contains water. Nails or pins of phosphor bronze will be driven through the band to hold the bristles in place and the band joint will be soldered. The fixing has to be extra strong to resist the enormous pressure, as the bristles swell up when they become wet. Such a brush would be very expensive – getting on for as much as £20 perhaps.

However, not all wall brushes come up to those standards of quality. For instance, to keep the price down to a reasonable level, some have hairs that are not entirely of bristle but include cheaper materials as well. This is known as a mixture brush. Right at the bottom of the price scale it is common for the band to be made of nickle-plated steel with an interlocked joint, and the pins could be of stainless steel, or even omitted altogether.

There is no need for you to go to the expense of buying the highest-quality wall brush, but do try to get a good one. Don't worry if you have to make do with a mixture brush – it will suit you admirably – but try to afford one that has a copper band nailed in place.

→ **Before you use a wall brush, flick and pull the bristles gently so that any loose ones will be dislodged, and not come out when you are painting. Then rinse the brush thoroughly in clean water. Not** only does this get rid of dust and loose particles, but it also helps to stop the paint from drying on the bristles.

Everybody knows, of course, that you wash emulsion paint out of the bristles of a wall brush with water, but not all do-it-yourselfers realize that you should do this when you knock off work for even a short while – for a meal, for instance. The reason for this is that emulsion paint can dry and harden in the stock very quickly and be very difficult to remove. Shake the brush out thoroughly before you start work again.

Flat Varnish Brushes

The brush you use for applying gloss paint is known as a flat varnish brush. It got its name because at one time there were no gloss paints, and a coat of varnish was applied over paint to impart a sheen and add extra protection. The brush used for applying this was known, not unnaturally, as a varnish brush. It was, however, round, because it was easier to make that way. Then modern methods of manufacture allowed brushes of the present shape to be made, and the term flat varnish brush was coined.

Two types of handle are found on flat varnish brushes. one is known as the beaver tail, and the other is called the American pattern. No one is sure how these terms originated.

A good flat varnish brush should always be made of pure bristle – do not compromise with a mixture brush here – and the best have a nickel-plated ferrule (it's known as a ferrule on a varnish brush, but a band on a wall brush). The bristles should be full and strong with a soft tip suitable for spreading and laying off gloss finishes (you will see what all this means when you come to the section on applying gloss paints on pages 57–60). The outside bristles should be slightly shorter than those in the centre so that the brush tapers slightly towards its tip.

However, the tip itself should be full and straight.

→ **When you are buying a varnish brush, examine it carefully, and open up its bristles. Look how much hair and how much timber are visible.** On very poor-quality varnish brushes, wedges are driven into the stock to thicken out the apparent amount of bristle, and you should look for these. Look, too, at the hairs in the centre, for it is here that the cheaper materials are placed. Whatever bristle a cheap brush has will be on the outside, for it is stronger than fibre and hair and stops the hair from flopping about. However, do not condemn a wall brush because it has a wedge. For here a wedge brings the tip of the bristle to a knife-like edge, and allows you to get into the stock of the brush to clean out the emulsion paint.

How many varnish brushes do you need? Nowhere near as many as you might imagine. For interior work you will probably get away with two sizes – 50-mm and 25-mm (2- and 1-in.). The 50-mm would be used for large areas such as doors, and the 25-mm for door and window frames etc. However, if you have Georgian-style windows with lots of panes and many small glazing bars it might be a good idea to get a 19-mm ($\frac{3}{4}$-in.) brush.

As you can see, varnish brushes are nowhere near as big as wall brushes. Therefore the objections about them being heavy when fully loaded are nowhere near as strong, so you could reasonably use a top-quality one. Moreover, since this type of brush is used with gloss paints, which need to be 'worked' more than the emulsions that are applied with wall brushes, you do need a good-quality tool. So I would suggest that you pick the best from a do-it-yourself shop's range, but go for middle quality in a trade outlet.

The same kit would do for woodwork out of doors unless you have large areas to deal with – on garage doors, for instance. In that case it would be as well to buy a 150-mm (3-in.) brush, too. Since, however, this tool will be used for coarser work, you can get away with a cheaper brush, and accordingly lower your standards when choosing it.

A professional uses a brand new brush only on ←
primers and undercoats, for that runs it in properly for use with top coats, smoothing down the bristles to a firm soft tip. And before starting work he always flexes the bristles through his hands to get rid of loose ones. A varnish brush should, however, never be soaked in water in the way that a wall brush is.

The Door Jamb Duster

One other brush that the top tradesmen consider indispensable is the door jamb duster, which they use for dusting off woodwork before they apply paint. Dust is the chief enemy of a really first-class finish, and will mar the final appearance of your work if you do not get rid of it. You may think that you can make do with a rag, or even an ordinary paintbrush, but neither of these is as effective as a jamb duster. In fact there is even a risk that they will force the dust into the surface instead of flicking it off.

How to Hold a Brush

The two types of paintbrush are held in entirely different ways. **To grip the flat varnish brush, you do not use** ←
the handle at all. Instead, you hold it by the ferrule, your four fingers on one side and your thumb on the other. That way you are able to flex your wrist and stroke the paint properly in both directions.

If, you may well ask, the handle is not used, why bother to have one at all? Several people have thought of that and experimented with the idea of a brush without a handle – obviously it would be cheaper to make. But the plain fact is that a handle is absolutely necessary for the

43

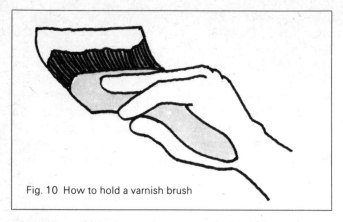

Fig. 10 How to hold a varnish brush

balance of the tool. Without one you cannot grip and control the brush properly.

On the other hand, you do use the handle to wield the wall brush. In fact, if you grip it just as though it were a ping-pong bat, you will not go far wrong. The reason for this is that when applying wall paints to large areas, you do use the brush in a sort of back- and forehand style, not unlike the action of stroking a ping-pong ball. But more of that later on.

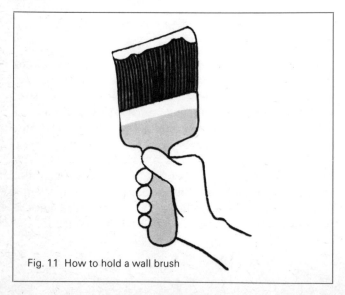

Fig. 11 How to hold a wall brush

The Painting Sequence

If you will be painting every surface in your room – the walls and ceiling, as well as the woodwork – then you should start with the ceiling, go on to the walls, and do the woodwork last. The reason for this is that you are more likely to splash the woodwork when working up high on ceiling and walls, than to splash the plaster when applying the gloss. If you do get splashes of emulsion paint on the woodwork, you should remove them before applying your gloss paint, for they may well show through. Wipe them off immediately with a rag, or flick them off with a scraper if you do not notice them until they have dried.

But if you intend to have a mixture of paint and paper you should do all the painting first. That way you do not have to worry about splashing newly hung paper with paint, and you need not bother to 'cut in' properly during your painting – ie to get a neat dividing line where paint and paper will meet. For you can let the paint stray on the wall as it will, and get a neat join by trimming the paper accurately.

Woodwork

Even though the woodwork is painted last, I will deal with it here first, for it is the most complicated.

Knotting

If the surfaces are bare, examine them to see if there are any knots or resinous areas. Unless these are sealed they will 'weep' through the finished work, and discolour the surface. You seal knots etc. with a liquid called, appropriately enough, knotting, which is brushed on.

It may well be that your existing paintwork suffers ← **from discoloration caused by the oozing of resin from knots, precisely because these were not treated with knotting when the wood was last painted. This does not mean that the paint must be stripped off –**

always provided that it is otherwise in good condition. For knotting does not need to go on bare
wood: you can apply it on top of the existing finish,
and it will protect subsequent coats that are applied.

Primer

But let's get back to bare timber. Having applied the
knotting, your next job is to brush on a primer. Many do-
it-yourselfers like to think that they can do without a
primer, but you will not get such a good finish if you omit
it. A primer provides an essential base for the rest of your
paintwork. On wood, it fills the grainy surface of the
timber and seals it, provides a key for subsequent coats
and helps to cushion them against movement in the
timber, and, finally, plays an important part in protecting
the timber against damp and moisture.

Undercoat

If you will be applying a liquid gloss as the finish,
then for the best results on top of the primer you
should apply an undercoat. At one time undercoats
were always said to be essential with gloss paint, but
in recent years they have fallen out of favour, and it is
true that with the development of extremely dense
pigments in gloss paints they are not as essential as
they used to be. However, you still get a better finish
if you use one, and in many instances one undercoat
and one coat of gloss will be better than two coats of
gloss.

The instructions on a tin of gloss have usually in the
past said that it was advisable to use with it only the same
brand of undercoat. There may well have been a large
element of sales talk in this – the manufacturers were
trying to bump up the sales of their own undercoat. But
now that so many paints are formulated in different ways
it is important to use the same brand of undercoat and
finishing paint, for only then can you be sure that they

will be compatible.

The undercoat always used to be a close match in colour to the top coat, and in many cases this is still true today. However, this colour matching is no longer necessary – once again because the pigments in modern top coats have much more obliterative power than they used to. Many of the better craftsmen will not specify a close-matching undercoat, for when the colours of the two paints are too similar you can easily miss a bit when you come to apply the top coat. As a result, whiskers of undercoat will be left exposed. Why does this matter? Because undercoat does not wear as well as a top coat.

If you are using a thixotropic gloss, undercoats do not apply, and you can brush on your top paint coat upon coat as needed, until you get a finish that suits you. Normally two are sufficient, but you can go to three for a really top-quality job.

Painting on Paint

Now let us suppose that you are decorating on top of an existing finish that was good enough not to need stripping during the preparation. Once again, if you have decided on a liquid gloss, it is a good idea to specify an undercoat first. Undercoats have a lot of body that will help to fill in small surface defects and leave a slightly textured surface, providing a good key for the top coat. And if the only defect in the existing surface is a fine crazing, then often an undercoat will act as a good enough barrier between that and the top coat. Also, if the old paint has weathered unevenly, the finishing gloss could sink into it in patches due to the extra suction, and there would be a loss of sheen. An undercoat will usually prevent this, too. However, if there are bare patches here and there, these should be touched-in with a primer first.

Once again, with gel paints an undercoat is not necessary and you merely apply them coat on coat.

Metal is treated in pretty much the same way as

woodwork, except that obviously there are no knots to be treated, and you must start off with a primer suitable for metal. Then you follow on just as though it were woodwork you were dealing with.

Rubbing Down Between Coats

Always, when applying gloss paints, you should give a light rub down with glasspaper between coats – primers, undercoats, the lot. This is not so much to apply a key – modern gloss paints don't really need one – but to get rid of any imperfections in your previous coat. At the very least, you will probably find that specks of dust have settled on your work, and sanding will get rid of these.

Walls and Ceiling

Now let us move on to the walls and ceiling.

Dealing with New Plaster

Not often as a do-it-yourselfer will you be called upon to tackle new plaster, for even if you move into a brand-new house the builder will usually have applied a coat or two of emulsion before handing the building over to you. Unless you were in on the deal at a very early stage, and were able to select your own decorations, the colour will probably be a neutral one, designed to cause offence to no one, and you may want to alter it. In that case, you treat it merely as a normal redecoration.

However, you may well have had a lot of renovation work done in an old house, or, indeed, an extension built in a new one, and that will leave you new plaster to deal with. This must be left to dry out thoroughly before you put a decorative surface on it. And that means waiting for at least six weeks, and preferably three months. If you ignore this warning, you risk the paint losing its opacity, starting to discolour, and even flaking off.

As the plaster dries out, you may get a white powdery deposit on the surface, the technical name for which is efflorescence. On no account should you try to wash this off, because it is dampness that caused it in the first place, and if you wet the plaster again you will only make things worse. Instead, you should wipe or brush it off with a stiff brush, then wait. The condition should eventually cure itself as the plaster dries out. If it does not, then you have a damp problem somewhere in the walls of your house, and you should call in a builder.

The other occasion on which you might be faced with raw plaster would be in a room whose walls have always been papered, and which you are deciding for the first time to paint. In this case just ordinary preparation would be called for.

Applying Emulsion Paint

Primers are not necessary on bare plaster, nor do emulsions have an undercoat. On bare surfaces, however, or one that is highly absorbent, you can thin the first coat of emulsion with water – but make sure that it is clean. The instructions on the tin usually give you details of quantities to use when thinning.

One of the advantages of emulsion paint is that it dries very quickly, and you can soon put the second coat on top of the first. In the case of new plaster, however, it is a good idea to leave the first coat to dry overnight.

When you are dealing with walls that have already been treated with emulsion paint, examine them first to see if they are powdery. Rub the palm of your hand over the surface to see if a powder deposit is left. Or stick a short length of Sellotape on the surface and see if any of the paint comes away when you peel the tape off. Should any of these tests reveal a powdery surface, after washing the surface treat it with a coat of stabilizing solution. When this has dried you can go on to paint in the normal way.

Emulsion paint that is not powdery can, once the normal preparation has been carried out, have coat on

49

coat of the new colour applied until you have achieved a satisfactory surface. In general you will find that two coats will be all that are required, and only in the case of a very marked colour change will you need three.

The Priming Coat

When you paint wood or metal that is at present bare, you need in general to start off with a primer. But it is important to choose the correct one. For a primer is a paint designed to stick to bare surfaces – whereas gloss coats and undercoats might not – and provide a foundation suitable to receive whatever finish you have chosen. The right primer also seals the surface to stop it being too porous, binds down a loose, flaking one, and on iron and steel inhibits rust.

Now the subject of primers is a very complicated one, and in discussing it we are in some ways leaving the field of the decorator and entering that of the paint technologist. In fact, faced with a real problem surface, the tradesman might well ring up the technical department of the company whose paint he is using to ask for advice, and there is no reason why you should not do the same – you will find you will be very well received. However, there are many things that the decorator knows about primers from experience, so let me explain them to you. By and large, they will be more than enough for you in your normal decorating.

But first one word of warning. Lots of primers are labelled multi-purpose or all-purpose or universal. These are very useful when you are dealing with lots of different surfaces during one bout of decorating, or when, for instance, you have tiny areas of metal mixed up among a lot of timber – eg screws or nails in some item of carpentry that you have just made. But 'multi' does not necessarily mean 'every', so when buying one of these primers do look at the instructions to make sure it is right for the surface you have in mind. When dealing with just one surface, it is always better to use the specialist primers intended for the job.

Timber

First let us deal with timber. Any knots should be treated with knotting (see page 45), then you can apply one of the conventional white or pink oil-based wood primers. In general these are non-toxic – ie they do not contain lead. But brands that contain lead are available and you might like to use them out of doors, where they will offer stronger protection. Be very wary of them, however. The new multi-purpose primers are also suitable for timber, and on interior work so are the primer undercoats. These latter are acrylic, water-based products – not unlike emulsion paints – so they dry very quickly, and the obvious advantage is that they speed up the whole process of redecoration, for in no time at all you can be applying your top coats.

Some softwoods are resinous. You can recognize them for they will feel very sticky to the touch, and you will see orange streaks which are resin oozing out. These timbers need an aluminium primer, and it is not a bad idea to treat very resinous areas with knotting first.

Plywood, blockboard and chipboard should be treated just like timber, and on hardboard use an all-purpose primer, or a primer-undercoat. Insulation boards, however, tend to be very porous, so use a primer sealer. If you come across any asbestos in your home, this, too, should be treated with a primer sealer before you paint. Never, incidentally, rub asbestos with glasspaper, and don't even dust it off, for you might release dangerous particles of it into the air. Instead, wash it down with clean water, then wrap the rag you have used in a polythene bag and throw it away.

Metals

Now over to metals. The traditional metal primers tend to

be toxic, so you might want to settle instead for a multi-purpose primer, especially since in most homes there will be only small areas of metal in among a lot of woodwork – eg metal window frames set in outer wooden ones.

Aluminium is now to be found in increasing quantities in our homes – on new window frames for instance, and especially if you have had double glazing fitted. If you wish to paint it, do not use a lead-pigmented metal primer, but settle for an all-purpose primer instead.

One problem metal you will come across is copper – you get it in water and central heating pipes. In general, copper is best left unpainted, but you may well want to cover up old and ugly pipes. In such cases, no primer is recommended. just make sure the metal is clean and free from grease, then apply gloss paint directly to it.

Walls

Finally, walls. When you are going to put emulsion paint on top of sound, dry plaster, there is no need for any sort of primer. You merely apply the emulsion coat on coat, although it is a good idea to thin down the first one with water according to the manufacturer's instructions. The same goes for cement, concrete, brickwork, etc., and when you are applying emulsion paint on top of lining papers and Anaglypta. However, on top of old emulsion paint that is powdery or flaking, you should use a primer-sealer. It is a good idea, too, to use a primer-sealer after you have removed whitewash or non-washable distemper from a wall.

Opening the Tin

You might think that it is an insult to your intelligence to devote a section to opening a paint tin, but there are one or two things to observe. First, when you take the can from the shelf – whether it is newly bought from the shop or not – you should dust it thoroughly, or any dust on the can might get into the paint and spoil the end result.

Next, how are you going to open the tin? Many tradesmen use a coin, although I must confess that I do not have a lot of success with this method myself. Many do-it-yourselfers use a screwdriver, which works, but you have ruined the tool for any further high-class carpentry. **The implement I use is the small tool that is** ◄— **sold for piercing cans of orange juice and the like. At one time these were given away free in off-licences because they were used for piercing cans of beer. Now that brewers and soft-drink manufacturers have gone over to pull-ring opening for their cans, you have to buy them at ironmongers.** You use the piercer upside down, of course – ie you place it on the edge of the can with the point upwards and under the rim of the lid. Lever, and the lid will come off easily. It works perfectly, except perhaps with the largest cans of all, which the do-it-yourselfer would be least likely to use.

Before opening the can, however, you should always read the instructions on the tin, for if you delay doing that until after it is opened, paint might run down the sides, and obliterate them.

Why Bother with a Paint Kettle?

The professional decorator does not work from the tin in which he buys his paint. Instead he pours the paint into a kettle, and uses that. I am sure you probably feel that this is an item of equipment you can manage very well without. And so you can – 99·9 per cent of amateur decorators do not bother with one. And yet that could well be one of the reasons why their work is not as good as they would like it to be. Certainly the tradesman is fully aware of the value of a good kettle.

So . . . why bother with a paint kettle? Why not just use the paint straight out of the tin? If you were always dealing with brand-new paint, just opened, then maybe you would get away with it. But gradually, towards the end of the day, you will find a build-up of hard paint forming on the rim of the can. You can pick up small flecks of this as you load your brush – some of them even get dislodged and fall into the paint – and these will be transferred on to your work. And you know what a problem it is wiping them off. You will avoid this if at the start of the session you pour new paint into a kettle.

In any case, when you are using paint from a can that has been opened previously, you have to strain it to get rid of old skin, and that means pouring it into another receptacle. You might as well use the proper thing. You could make do with an old jam jar – provided that you have one wide enough to take your brush. But how will you hold it? By grabbing the outside with the palm of your hand? Well, let's hope it doesn't slip through when the palm of your hand is covered with paint, as it inevitably will be – especially when you are at the top of a ladder.

Paint kettles were traditionally metal, but now you can get plastic ones. These are much cheaper, and they are easier to scrape clean afterwards. You can, for instance, flex them so that the paint film cracks and falls away from the surface.

To clean the traditional metal kettle, painters take it out of doors well away from harm, soak a rag in paraffin, place the rag in the kettle and set fire to it. This burns off the paint film. Any remaining paint can be scraped off, and the kettle cleaned with abrasive paper.

→ **There is a correct way to hold a paint kettle in your hand. Its handle should lie in the fingers of your hand, but your forefinger should extend along and under it. When you want to charge your brush, you stretch out this forefinger, which will pivot the kettle out of the way of your hand, giving you plenty of access to the paint.**

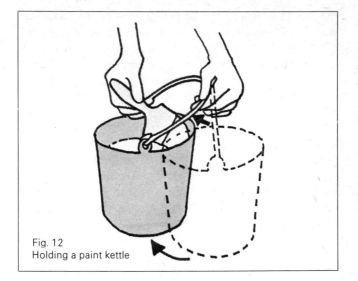

Fig. 12
Holding a paint kettle

Straining the Paint

If the can of paint you are about to use has never been opened before, the paint inside will not need straining. But if it has been used then almost certainly there will be hard paint and skin that you must get rid of if you are to have a tip-top finished result.

Paint hardens when it comes into contact with the air. You may read tips that you can stop skin from forming by storing a tin upside-down – the theory being that with the lid at the bottom covered by paint air will not be able to enter. Unfortunately, there will be enough air already inside the can to react on the paint – and when you turn the tin the right way up the skin will be in the worst possible place: at the bottom.

So always store your paint with the tin the right way up, and the lid fixed firmly in place, so that only the air already inside will reach the paint.

When you open a can of paint, stir it thoroughly, making sure you mix in all the sediment at the bottom of the can. However, if the tin is fairly empty, and has been standing for some time, you may well find that there is a thick layer of skin all over the top of the paint. Try to cut this off intact, like a cake, with a knife, keeping as close to the sides of the tin as possible so that little will be left clinging there. Then stir the rest. Now you must strain the paint, and a pair of old nylon tights is still the best thing to use. Some experts say that you should use the tights to cover the top of the tin from which you are pouring; others that you should put the tights over the kettle. I suggest that you experiment, and choose whichever method you feel happiest with. The strained paint should be free of all sediment, and you can start to use it immediately.

If you are using a thixotropic paint, you will see a notice on the tin warning you not to stir it, and in general you should follow this advice. If there is any liquid on top of the paint in a previously opened can, pour it away. If the paint seems in very bad condition you can stir it after removing whatever layer of skin lies on the top. Strain the liquid, then put it on one side to stand for a day. It will then re-solidify, and once more be ready for use.

Paints that are Dangerous

At one time paints contained lead, which is, of course, a poison and if taken internally can have dangerous, not to say fatal, consequences. The danger is not only to the decorator who is applying the paint – think of a child biting at the bars of a cot or a toy that has been treated with lead-based paints, or a pet gnawing at woodwork. However, there is no need to worry. Practically all modern paints, especially those that are available over the retail counter, are non-toxic and you can use them anywhere in your home with complete safety.

However, some paints with dangerous quantities of lead are available to the trade, and many decorators will tell you that they offer the best protection for woodwork, particularly out of doors. This is especially true of some primers. There is no reason why you should not apply these paints, provided you are fully aware of the sort of material you are handling. Keep the paints well away from children and pets, and confine them to areas of your home well out of harm's way. While you are painting keep your hands away from your mouth – a warning that applies particularly to smokers.

However, most do-it-yourselfers will feel, like me, that the safe non-toxic paints offer all the protection that is needed, and will stick to these.

Applying a Liquid Gloss

A liquid gloss, although it gives the best finish, is the most difficult of all the paints to apply, which is why I will deal with it first. Having mastered the art of applying this with a brush, you will be better able to understand the principles of painting.

Dust is the big enemy of a good gloss finish, so at the beginning you should make sure there is none lying around on the floor – sweep it well, or better still vacuum clean it first. Also, avoid wearing woollen clothing from which loose fibres could fall on to the work. **Finally, just before you begin, rub your palms over the surface – 'palm the work off' in the jargon of the trade. The slight dampness of your skin will pick up any loose bits of dirt.**

You start the actual painting by loading your brush, and to do so you should dip its bristles to about a third of their depth into the liquid. Aim to submerge them each time to the same depth so that you always get an equal amount of paint on them. Then press the bristles first against one side of the container, then against the other, to squeeze out surplus paint. You will find it easier to do this in a kettle than in a paint can – yet another reason in favour of using the proper receptacle. Now you are ready to begin.

Let us imagine for a start that you are painting a largish flat area – a flush door would be the most obvious example (although I shall be dealing with doors separately later on), and that you are right-handed; you will work the opposite way around if you are left-handed. **Begin at the left-hand side of the door, but bring your brush into contact with the work 25–50 mm (1–2 ins) short of the top. If you begin right at the top paint will bubble over on to the top, then flow back and you will get an unsightly build-up of paint – you will, in the words of the tradesman, 'pick up a thick edge'.** Apply the paint from the top of the door down to about waist height, using upward and downward

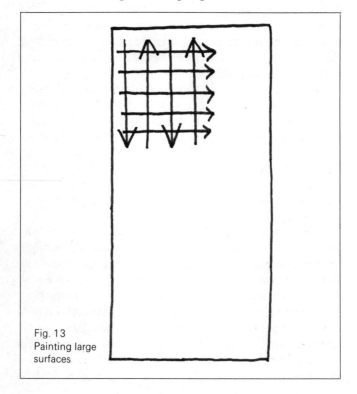

Fig. 13
Painting large
surfaces

strokes. Hold the brush as explained in the previous section, and flex it against the work which will cause the paint held in the bristles to flow down to the narrow tip of the brush. Remember that a gloss paint needs to be applied liberally in a full-flowing coat. Don't dab your brush at the work as though you were trying to stab someone. It should approach the work gently in an arc, like an aeroplane coming in to land.

When you have covered about 200–300 mm (9–12 ins) of the width of the door, then, without reloading the brush, spread the paint out evenly with a series of horizontal strokes across the original vertical ones – a process known, not unnaturally, as cross brushing. This guards against the possibility of unsightly 'tears' and runs. Finally, without further charging your brush with paint, make a series of light-as-a-feather strokes in the original vertical direction. And this process the trades-man calls laying off. **The laying off should be done very** ← **gently and delicately. Your brush should be at an angle to the work, and just its bristles should touch the paint. Take great care over laying off. It is the finishing touch that stamps the final seal of quality on your work.**

Having dealt with this first section of the door, you can go on to the next one immediately to the right of it. This you will deal with in exactly the same way, but make sure during your cross brushing that you carry your strokes right into the paint on the first section. Continue in this way until you have finished the entire width of the door. Then you should carry out a final cross brushing of all the paint you have applied.

With the top band of the door completed, you can now go on to the one underneath – most people would split the average door into three horizontal bands, but you might make do with two. However many you decide on, treat them all in the same way that I have described for the top one, but carry your vertical strokes – both those for the original application of paint and the laying-off ones – into the top band of paint, otherwise you will get a hard, visible edge where the various sections meet. Similarly, the horizontal strokes of your cross brushing should go into the neighbouring paint.

Finally, when the whole panel is finished, give a final laying off, and stand back and examine your work to make sure the entire surface is covered, and that there are no runs. Then you can regard the job as finished.

On long, narrow stretches of wood – skirting boards and door frames, for instance – such a technique is obviously not called for. All you have to do is make sure the paint is well spread, so that there will be no runs, and each time you reload your brush after it has run dry, carry your first strokes well into the paint already there, so that you will not get a hard join line showing.

Applying a Gel Gloss

You treat a gel gloss very like a liquid one, but when you charge your brush there is no need to press it on the sides of the kettle to get rid of surplus paint.

You apply the gel in pretty much the same way, too, except that you have to be aware of over-brushing. For a gel paint functions merely because pressure from your brush causes it to turn liquid. When you first dip your brush into the kettle, the paint that it touches turns liquid, and clings to its bristles. As you withdraw the brush, the paint solidifies again (which is why there are fewer drips with this type of paint). When you brush the paint on to the wood, it will again turn liquid, allowing you to spread it out, and it will turn solid once more as your brush leaves it. **If you overdo the brushing out, then the gel will be too liquid, and you will lose the big advantage of a gel gloss (which is, of course, that it is less likely to run than a liquid one, and so you can apply it more thickly). So with a gel gloss you must aim for less cross brushing and laying off.**

Applying Undercoats and Primers

These paints are applied in a manner fairly similar to the way you brush on gloss. However, they are not so free flowing, so there is less risk of runs. This is particularly true of primer going on a bare surface. Therefore laying off is not so important. **However, it is vital to ensure that these paints are applied evenly, to give a good base for the top coats. In the case of a wood primer, brush it hard against the bare surface, almost forcing it into the bare timber.**

Painting a Door

There are two distinct types of door to be found in British homes – flush and panelled. **Whichever type of door you have, before you start to paint it you should first of all remove all the 'furniture' – handles, catches,**

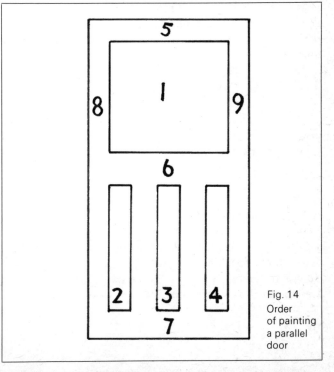

Fig. 14
Order
of painting
a parallel
door

etc. – that you do not want to be coated with paint. **It is definitely quicker to remove the furniture and replace it when you have finished than try to paint round it.** When I have finished painting I always replace the handle straightaway – if you take great care over this you can manage it without disturbing the paint – so that I can open and close the door immediately. Some people, however, prefer to wait for the paint to dry before re-fixing everything. In that case, it is a good idea to drive a wooden peg into the hole for the handle so that you can operate the door without touching the paint.

Anyway, on to the actual painting. A flush door is dealt with as already explained for large areas (see page 57). The order for painting the various parts of a panelled door is shown in Figure 14.

Incidentally, do you know which colour the edges of a door should be painted? The rule is quite simple: the edge nearest to the handle should be painted the same colour, and at the same time, as the side that opens into the room. The hinge edge should be treated as part of the other side of the door, which may well be a different colour.

How to 'Cut In'

'Cutting in' is the term the tradesman applies to getting a neat join where paints of a different colour meet – ie the angle between a coloured wall and a white ceiling, or where paint meets a different decorative material, as for instance the join between paint on a kitchen cabinet and the plastic worktop.

Where there is a definite angle at the point where the colours or materials meet, as in the examples given above, then cutting in is easy to achieve. **Load your brush lightly, place it on the work about 3 mm ($\frac{1}{8}$ in.) away from the edge, then slowly and gradually push it along to meet the joint. Now press lightly on the brush, so that it will not wander about, and firmly**

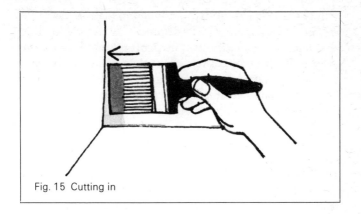

Fig. 15 Cutting in

draw it along, to make a straight line. It sounds easy, and it is easy, once you have a little practice.

Some cutting in, is however, more complicated than this – where, for instance, there is an abrupt colour change in the middle of a wall, as in some modern designs where a wall might be decorated in several bands of different colour. The only way to achieve a good break here is with masking tape.

Decorator's masking tape is self-adhesive, and you stick it down in place where you want your neat join to be. It is a good idea to go over it with a seam roller (see section on wallpapering tools on page 80) so that you can be sure it is firmly stuck down, and paint will not be able to creep under the edges. Apply your paint making sure you come right up to the edge of the tape, and straying on to it if necessary. Let the paint dry thoroughly before tearing off the tape. You will then see a very neat join. Incidentally, don't try to make do with ordinary sticky tape. It simply won't work.

Painting Window Frames
One obvious instance of cutting in occurs when you paint window frames. In books aimed at do-it-yourselfers, you

63

will read of several dodges designed to make it easier for the amateur to paint window frames – from masking tape to shields of various kinds. **The professional knows that proper cutting in is the quickest and easiest method of dealing with window frames. I would urge you to adopt the same course. A few practice runs, and you will find it very easy to cut in properly.**

The window frames are the part of the interior woodwork that has to stand up to the most exacting conditions, for you get a lot of condensation on them, and, if there is no radiator under the window, they are in the coldest part of the room. So take great care of the frames and do the job properly. They need to be well prepared in the first place, and you must carry out your painting thoroughly.

Do not cut in right to the edge of the glass, but allow a thin strip of paint – say 3 mm ($\frac{1}{8}$ in.) wide – on the pane as protection for the putty.

Applying Emulsion Paint

Emulsions are the easiest of all paints to work with, which is why they are so popular. No need to worry about smoothing the paint out, cross brushing or laying off. Basically, all you do is load your brush, bring it to the work, then spread the paint out in all directions, making sure you cover the area evenly and thoroughly.

An emulsion paint can cause runs, just like gloss, so you have to take care that it is well brushed out, but the complicated brushwork associated with gloss paint is not called for.

Painting a Ceiling

Many do-it-yourselfers attempt to paint a ceiling from just a pair of ordinary household steps, and in so doing I think they make a very big mistake. For they thus turn what is anyway a tiring and tedious job into an absolutely exhausting one. The area of ceiling you can reach from the top of the steps is very limited, and you have to get down continually from them to move them on to the next spot. To paint a ceiling properly, safely and without undue exertion you must have a scaffold board (see page 15).

In most normal-sized rooms you will be able to cover a ceiling completely from just three positions of your scaffold board, you will have finished the job in a small fraction of the time it takes from a pair of steps, and will feel much fresher into the bargain.

You should paint a ceiling in strips parallel to the ← **wall containing the largest window. So set up your scaffold parallel to this wall, and just far enough away from it to be able to reach the end of the ceiling. Paint from this position a strip as wide as you can comfortably reach, then move your scaffold and go on to tackle the next strip.** In no circumstances try to make the far edges of the strips a neat straight line, because the joins between the strips will show. You should aim for a ragged effect, and carry the paint from one patch well into the next. Working from a scaffold you will find that the edge of the first strip will still be wet when you come to paint alongside it. Its 'wet edge will still be live' is how the tradesman would express it. You will therefore be able to carry the new paint well into it. If you were working from steps, the first strip might well have hardened when you came back to it. So you would get a hard line between the various strips, which could be visible as what the professionals call a 'lap' mark in the finished result.

When painting the ceiling, there is no need to ← **attempt any cutting in – ie trying to get a good, sharp, dividing line where the ceiling meets the top of the walls. Just make sure the ceiling itself is properly covered, and if the walls are to be a different colour, then you can go for your neat join when painting them.**

Painting a ceiling is a hard, demanding job – like any work where you have to keep your hands stretched up high – but try to keep at it to finish it in one go, so that you always have a live, wet edge to pick up. Have a rest when the job is finished.

If you are elderly or have a weak heart it might be better for you not to paint the ceiling. You could ask a friend or relative to do it for you, or call in a professional. You can decorate the rest of the room yourself, but if you are in any doubt on this point ask your doctor's advice. But painting a ceiling is, of course, well within the scope of the young and healthy.

Painting the Walls

Walls should be painted in a series of horizontal strips, and you begin each strip at the source of light, which means the window end in the case of walls at right angles to the window wall, and near a subsidiary source of light, such as a door or secondary window, for other walls. You should aim to work on each wall fairly quickly, for emulsion paint (which is what you will nearly always be applying on a wall) dries much more quickly than other paints, and, as when tackling a ceiling, it is important to keep the wet edge live in order to avoid lap marks. If you find yourself getting tired you would do better to keep going and have your rest when each individual wall is complete. But painting a wall is not so demanding as tackling a ceiling, and you should be all right.

→ **Again, as with a ceiling, don't let the bottom of the strip end in a rigid, straight line, but make it a ragged one instead, as another insurance against lap marks showing through.**

You will work more quickly if you tackle the top of the wall from a scaffold board rather than a pair of steps. Set your board at a height that allows you just comfortably to reach the top of the wall. If the ceiling is of a different colour, then first of all do your cutting in using a fairly narrow brush – 25-mm (1-in.) is fine, but some decorators think they get along better with a 50-mm (2-in.) one. Then paint the top horizontal strip, making it of a depth you can conveniently manage without stooping, which would be tiring. Then remove your scaffold board, tackle the next strip, and finally the one or two others that will be necessary to complete the average-sized wall. At the top of each strip, carry the vertical strokes of your brushwork well into the paint above – you will be able to do this if the wet edge is still live – to avoid a rigid dividing line showing between them.

At one time it was fashionable to have the walls of a room in different colours. This is not nearly so popular now, but if you intend using more than one colour always put the lighter one on first and don't bother about cutting in neatly. Just make sure you cover the entire area fully and allow the paint to stray on to the neighbouring surface as it will. Then do your cutting in when you come to apply the darker colour, which will obliterate more easily.

I have stressed the importance of a live, wet edge when painting with emulsion much more than I have with gloss paint. There are two reasons for this. In the first place emulsion paint dries much more quickly than gloss. In most ways this is a big advantage, for it means that you can finish off decorating a room much more quickly. Nevertheless, you have to get a move on when using it to make sure there will always be a wet edge to pick up. Secondly, you are normally dealing with much larger areas, so the edge could have dried when you come to pick it up again.

The consequences of the wet edge going off would be more serious with gloss – the lap mark would be harder and more visible. But it is not so likely to happen, because the paint takes longer to dry, and you are coating a much smaller area.

Painting with a Roller

At one time you could never have included a section on paint rollers in a book describing professional ways of decorating, for the tradesman simply did not use them. In fact, the do-it-yourselfer was way ahead of him in recognizing the advantages of this tool. But now the professionals have come to accept it and you will frequently see them using a roller. The advantage of a roller is that, although you can never achieve as good a surface as you will with a brush, especially when applying gloss paint, it is an extremely useful device for covering large areas quickly, where it will give you a finish that is perfectly adequate. Once rollers were suited only to water-based paints, but they have been developed so that you can in fact now use them with gloss.

The covering of the roller, which actually applies the paint, is known as the sleeve and this is now generally removable so that you can clean it more easily, and also buy replacements when it has worn out. You can get sleeves made of plastic foam (the cheapest of all) or synthetic or natural fibres. Synthetic fibre sleeves – Dynel, Dacron and Nevel are common names – come in a variety of pile lengths, ranging from short stubble to a luxurious shaggy one. Among natural fibres, mohair and woolpile sleeves have a relatively short pile, but sheepskin is much longer. As for the price of fibre sleeves, the synthetics are the cheapest, closely followed by mohair, while sheepskin is the dearest of all.

Which of these you should use depends on what type of paint you are applying to which surface. For a start, you need a short-piled sleeve on smooth surfaces, and a long pile on the rough ones. Which means paint with foam, mohair, short woolpile or short synthetics on plaster, lining paper, wood, boards such as plywood and hardboard, metal etc., but with a sheepskin or a long synthetic pile on embossed wallpapers, Anaglyptas, brick, concrete and cement rendering.

However, there is a complication in that natural fibre sleeves, especially those with a long pile, tend to soak up the moisture from a water-based paint, and in so doing lose their natural resilience and paint-holding capacity. On the other hand, synthetic fibres are impervious to water, so you should use these with emulsion paints and water-based paints for outside walls, but the natural fibre sleeves for gloss paints (including eggshells and under-coats) and out of doors for oil-based masonry paint.

Rollers come in a range of widths, commonly from 150 mm (6 ins) to 250 mm (10 ins) in the do-it-yourself ranges, but longer when they are sold as tradesmen's tools. As with brushes, you will encounter the same contradiction that the bigger the tool, the less time you spend charging it and the more quickly you finish the job, but the more tiring it is to wield. You have to decide for yourself what size you think you can cope with.

Rollers must be loaded with paint from a tray. Both roller and tray can be bought separately, but it is usual to get them as kits, in which a small cutting-in brush is often included. Strain your paint from the can into the tray: some have a line indicating how much can go in, but

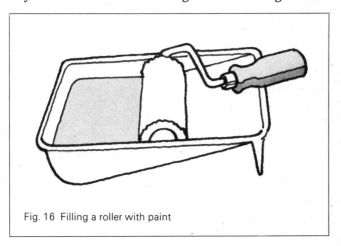

Fig. 16 Filling a roller with paint

otherwise leave about half of the sloping part uncovered. Push the roller into the deepest part of the tray, then roll it backwards and forwards on the slope to distribute the paint evenly throughout the sleeve, and squeeze out all the excess. Your aim should be to load the roller enough for it not to dry out too quickly, yet not so much that paint drips everywhere – you will soon find a happy medium.

→ **When you apply the roller to the work, make your first run upwards on a wall, and away from you on a horizontal surface. Roll it steadily and slowly, making sure the entire surface is covered. When the paint starts to run out recharge the roller immediately. Resist the temptation to make your paint go further by trying to squeeze that little bit extra from the roller. You will get a worse finish this way.**

Rollers cannot, of course, get too near an angle, and your cutting in here must be done with a small brush. If there isn't one in your roller kit, use your 25-mm (1-in.) gloss paint brush.

You may have read the tip that you can fit a broom handle to your roller so that you can tackle the ceiling while standing on the floor. There is another advantage, too, in that with the handle held at an angle the sleeve will not be directly overhead, so there is less risk of your being splashed by paint.

When you come to clean the sleeve, first roll out as much excess paint as you can on sheets of old newspaper. Then remove the sleeve, and wash it. Unless there are instructions to the contrary on the paint tin, you should clean oil paint out in paraffin, then wash the sleeve in detergent, finally giving it a good rinse. Emulsion paint can be cleaned from the sleeve with water.

You may think it quicker, incidentally, to leave the sleeve on the roller for this cleaning, but paint can get between sleeve and roller, harden, and make it impossible to take off the sleeve when it needs renewing.

Cleaning your Brushes

At the end of the session comes the job that most people hate – cleaning the brushes. But it is one you should not skip. Paintbrushes are expensive – even though you will not be paying as much for them as the tradesman – and a good one is worth taking care of to ensure that you get full value for the money you have spent. Professionals are very aware of the importance of cleaning brushes well, and they allow time for it at the end of the working day.

Gloss

The most difficult paint to clean out of your brush is gloss, and a wide range of proprietary products is sold to make things easier. **Most professionals, however,** ← **prefer to use a solvent that is comparatively inexpensive – paraffin. Stand your brush in an old jar, making sure it sits squarely on its bristles (if it is a good one there is no need to suspend it by means of a hole bored in its handle, for its bristles will be firm enough). Then pour in just enough paraffin to come to the top of the bristles. You can leave it like that overnight or even longer. When you want to start work again wash it out in clean paraffin, shake it thoroughly, then work it dry on a clean rag.**

When you have finished decorating, wash your brush out first in two changes of paraffin, then in soapy water, finally rinsing it out in clean water. Shake it thoroughly, or spin the handle between your hands, then dry it on a clean rag. The brush should be stored wrapped in paper – kitchen paper is ideal. Smooth the bristles neatly into place as you wrap, then put the brush out of harm's way flat on a shelf.

On no account should you ever store a brush wrapped in impervious materials, such as polythene, which stop the bristles drying out properly.

With some modern gloss paints, brush cleaning is much less trouble than that, and you clean them with a

71

solution of detergent in water. Always follow the instructions on the tin. It is, incidentally, a good idea to read these before you begin work, because paint might flood over the sides of the can and obliterate the instructions.

Varnish brushes should never be soaked in water. That would cause the bristles to swell up, and distort the shape of the brush.

Emulsion

Emulsion paint is cleaned out of a brush with water. Make sure, however, that you wash the brush even when you knock off work for a short break – a meal or tea break, for instance, as emulsion paint can harden in the stock while you work, and be very difficult to remove. Shake the brush thoroughly before you start work again.

3 Wallpapers

There are three reasons why you would choose to cover the walls of a room with paper rather than paint them. The first would be that you prefer pattern to large areas of plain colour. The second would be that paper will cover up bad wall surfaces, and finally, a papered wall is much warmer to the touch than a painted one. In fact, many people would say that it looks warmer, too, and makes the whole atmosphere of a home feel less wintry.

So you can see that wallpapers are particularly suited to an old house that is being renovated, because they cut down on the amount of preparation needed on the walls. In fact for some old plaster surfaces, papers are the only decorative finish you can consider, because the amount of filling and making good required would rule out paint.

The reverse side of the coin is that, in general, papers are a more expensive way of covering a wall, and, furthermore, many do-it-yourselfers feel that hanging wallpaper calls for much more skill than applying paint. In a way they are right, but it is not all that difficult to master the art of hanging wallpaper, and in this section I will show you exactly what you have to do.

The principles of wallpapering can be expressed in a nutshell. You cut the paper roughly to length, then paste it. Offer the paper up to the wall and brush it into place in the precise position it will occupy. While it is actually there, you mark it to fit. You then peel it away from the wall, cut it to the marks you have made, then smooth it back in position – wallpaper paste is made in such a way that it enables you to do this. And your paper is hung.

But between the theory and the practice there lie, for

the do-it-yourselfer, uncharted seas, where you will require help and guidance.

First Choose your Wallcovering

Before we begin to think of hanging wallpaper, we should look at the various types available. The choice (and here I am speaking only of types, not patterns) is not so wide and therefore nowhere near so confusing as it is with paints.

Basic Wallpapers

Right from the start, let us get our terminology correct. Many of the so-called 'wallpapers' that are used in our homes do not, in fact, consist of paper at all, so the trade tends to use the all-embracing term 'wallcovering' to cover the full range of decorative materials (other than, of course, paint) that are used on a wall.

However, ordinary wallpapers are, in fact, the most common type of wallcovering, and they offer the widest range of pattern. While some exclusive papers, particularly the hand-printed ones, carry price tags that put them right in the luxury class, wallpapers are by and large the cheapest form of wallcovering. In fact, at the lower end of the scale, they do not cost all that much more than emusion paint.

The big snag with ordinary papers is that you cannot really clean them. True, some of them are described as waterfast, but that means little more than that you can wipe off any paste that gets on the pattern during hanging. If you do have any accidents with an ordinary paper you can often remove spots of grease etc. by rubbing them gently with small lumps of bread. But anything in the nature of washing is right out.

However, don't be put off too much by these remarks. You can use these papers widely in homes where they are not likely to be subjected to the ravages of young children. But in a house full of children or animals they should be confined to adult bedrooms, or parts of the living room out of reach of sticky fingers.

Washable Papers

If you want a paper that you can clean, then you must go for a washable wallpaper. This is an ordinary printed wallpaper that has been coated with a thin film of plastic, so it is still in order to refer to it as a 'paper'. The amount of washing that washables will stand is, however, limited. You can wipe dirt from them with a soapy cloth, but beware of using too much force. Washables can be used on any surface that is likely to suffer from stains and splashes, but are not suitable for really heavy-duty areas.

Vinyls

For really hard wear and cleanability, you have to go for a vinyl. Here we meet up with the first of our wallcoverings that is not really a paper, for the colour, design and any surface texturing of a vinyl are all contained in a PVC film which is bonded to a paper backing only so that it can be handled more easily.

You can actually scrub vinyls without any fear of damaging or wearing away the surface of the design, so obviously they are ideal, not only for obvious trouble spots such as kitchens and bathrooms, but children's bedrooms and staircase walls as well.

The snag is, though, that they are expensive. Bear this in mind when deciding whether to choose one or not. Many people, in fact, hang a vinyl when they could get away with a washable wallpaper – especially if they like to change the decorations frequently.

Relief Decorations

Another group of widely used wallcoverings are known as relief decorations, because they have a design that is deeply embossed in them. This makes them highly suitable for covering up bad wall surfaces, and they are extensively used in the renovation of older properties. Most of them are manufactured by the Crown company, and the names I give in the following paragraphs are all Crown trade marks. However, similar products come from other companies, and some relief decorations are sold under store brand names.

These decorations usually have a white surface meant to be painted, so that the design possibilities are endless. You choose a pattern that appeals to you and give it whatever colour you wish.

The cheapest of the Crown relief decorations is Anaglypta, which consists of two layers of paper bonded together. Supaglypta looks similar but is made from cotton fibres rather than wood pulp, so it is stronger and the pattern can be more deeply embossed.

Vinaglypta is a relief decoration with a vinyl surface – in other words you get the hard-wearing qualities of a vinyl in addition to all the advantages of an embossed pattern. This, again, is more expensive.

Woodchip Paper
A type of paper that many people associate with relief decoration is woodchip paper. This consists of small chips of real wood sandwiched between two layers of paper in a random pattern. This, too, is ideal as a cover-up for bad walls, and has a surface that is meant to be painted. It is relatively cheap.

Hessian
Many amateur decorators like to use hessian because the fact that it has not got a real pattern means there is no bother of matching up. It also makes a durable and attractive wallcovering and is ideal for poor walls. Hessians come in a range of colours, and can also be painted. Always make sure that you buy a paper-backed hessian, designed for hanging on the wall. If you try to make do with a furnishing hessian (which is admittedly

cheaper) it will shrink as the glue dries out, and you will have unsightly gaps between the various lengths.

Flock
Real flock papers, as well as being ruinously expensive, are very delicate, and almost impossible for the do-it-yourselfer to handle successfully – in fact, many tradesmen will shy away from using them.

But vinyl flocks are a different thing altogether, being just as tough, and you can also wash these flocks just as easily as ordinary vinyl. There is no reason whatsoever why you should not try your hand at these.

Paperless 'Paper'
The latest form of wallcovering contains no paper at all. Made by ICI and known as Novamura, it is made from lightly foamed polythene. The big difference about it is that you paste the wall, not the material, and hang the Novamura from the roll. Novamura is easy to clean, to hang, and to strip off when you want to redecorate.

Luxury Papers
After this, we are getting into very specialist – and expensive – fields. For a start there are foils and metallic papers. These conduct electricity, so they should not be hung in bathrooms, or tucked behind light switches and socket outlets. And in the real luxury class comes a range of grasscloths, silks, suedes and so on. I do not think they are of any real concern to the ordinary home decorator.

The Right Surface
Like every other decorative material, wallcoverings must go on a suitable surface if they are to give their best. The ideal surface is a plaster wall that has always been wallpapered in the past, for then all you need do is strip off the old paper, as explained on page 19, and with the bare plaster exposed, hang your new paper. But you can

hang paper on a much wider range of surfaces than that. If you have a problem surface in your home, and you wish to cover it with paper, then get in touch with the manufacturer whose product you have chosen, and ask his advice.

Here are a few recommendations for coping with some of the surfaces you might meet in your home.

Emulsion-painted Surfaces
These need to be washed down, then sealed with a multi-purpose primer, thinned down according to the manufacturer's instructions. Size before hanging the paper. An emulsion with a high sheen needs to be stripped off with a chemical paint stripper, which is such a chore that it might deter you from choosing paper for that wall. A silk finish emulsion should be treated like gloss paint.

Gloss-painted Surfaces
The surface must be well washed to get rid of grease, rinsed, allowed to dry, then sized. Hang lining paper first. A very smooth, hard oil paint needs rubbing down to provide a key.

Distempered Surfaces
Non-washable distemper and old whitewash must be removed, as explained on page 26. With washable distempers, just scrape the surface to get rid of old, loose and flaking material, then apply a multi-purpose primer, which needs to be sized once it has dried. If the surface of a washable distemper is sound, it needs merely to be sized before you start hanging the paper.

Wallboards
Coat any screw or nail heads with a zinc chromate primer, then treat the board with wallboard primer. Size once the primer is dry. On very absorbent surfaces, such as

medium-density hardboards, you can apply size before the primer.

Concrete
This must be thoroughly washed down with detergent first, allowed to dry, then sized.

Polystyrene Wall Linings
These are often stuck to a wall to make it warmer, and thus less condensation-prone. The polystyrene should be treated with a lining paper, using a thick paste, and preferably one containing a fungicide, like those for use under vinyl, to inhibit mould growth.

How Much Will You Need?
You should always buy at the start as much paper as you will need to finish the room. If you don't order quite enough, and have to go back for an extra roll, you may find that it has come from a different printing batch, and a slight colour variation will show up when the paper is on the wall. (But see page 89 for what you do about this.) So how do you make sure you have enough?

Wallpaper shops have printed tables that help them to estimate the quantities required. They ask you to measure the height of your room, and its perimeter, and the table tells them how much you need. They ask you to include doors and windows in your perimeter measurements on the basis that this will ensure you have an extra allowance for trimming. It works after a fashion, but it is a bit rough and ready.

This is what the decorator does. First he measures the height of the wall to be papered – from skirting board to ceiling, or picture rail if there is one. He knows that wallcoverings in Britain come in standard rolls that are 10·05 m (33 ft.) long. So he is able to work out how many drops he will get out of a roll. In

deciding on the number of drops, he will take into account the size of the pattern, for you can get a lot of wastage in matching up a large repeat.

Next you have to find how many widths of paper will go round the room. No need for any measuring and complicated mathematics here. Use a spare roll of paper – it's 520 mm (20½ ins) wide, incidentally – as a measuring stick. Work out how many you will need by walking round the room and placing it on the wall. Ignore doors and windows in this measuring. Now divide the number of widths by the number of drops per roll, and you have the number of rolls required. Add a little extra for areas over doors, and around windows.

A ward of warning. Some continental and specialist papers can vary in size from the dimensions I have given above, so it is always wise to check.

The Tools You Need

Bucket and Stick
Your first requirements are an ordinary plastic bucket in which to mix your paste, and a clean stick to stir the mix as you add the paste powder to water.

Rule and Pencil
The paper must be cut to the correct length (and sometimes width, too) and for this some measuring device is needed. You probably already have a sprung steel tape or a dress making tape, but neither of these is ideal for the paper hanger. **When you are wallpapering many of the measurements you need will be horizontal ones, and these can be taken much more quickly if you have a rule that can be held rigid in one hand. The professional decorator tends to prefer a folding, boxwood rule.** Try to take a horizontal measurement with a sprung steel tape held in one hand, and watch it flop. After you have measured the paper, you need to

mark it, and for that you should use a pencil only.

Scissors

The paper will need cutting to size, and many people use a pair of dressmaking scissors. But remember, the longer the scissor blades, the straighter will be your cut. The scissors the tradesman uses are about 300 mm (12 ins) long, but I am sure you would find these unwieldy, and would be happier with something smaller and, of course, cheaper. I would say that 250 mm (10 ins) ought to be the maximum size of blade to go for, but you might even plump for blades as short as 175 mm (7 ins). However, you would find it difficult to cut wallpaper accurately with anything shorter than that. **Since a lot of the cutting is** ← **done while the paper is wet, scissors used in decorating pick up a lot of moisture. So buy a pair that are non-rusting – chromium-plated ones for instance. These are not easy to find in do-it-yourself shops, but if you hunt around, you should come across some.**

Knife

When you are working with vinyls, a retractable-bladed knife, such as the Stanley knife, can be used for the trimming, too.

Brush

The paste has to be brushed on to the paper, but there is no need to buy a special tool; the brush which you use for emulsion paint is perfectly satisfactory, and it is very easy to clean the old paste out of it when you have finished.

Don't make the mistake of choosing too big a brush – one with bristles about 75 mm (3 ins) long would be ideal. Anything bigger you would find too heavy to wield.

Pasting Table

The pasting has to be carried out somewhere, and the

professional uses a proper pasting table. This is a lightweight one that folds up, so that it can be easily carried around. Because they think they will not use it all that often, many do-it-yourself decorators try to skip buying a pasting table and use some substitute: taking a flush door from its hinges and using that on the kitchen table is a popular dodge. I think, though, that to do a professional-looking job you need the right equipment. The best way to economise on the price of a table is for two or three neighbours to get together to buy the table, each using it as required.

Steps

Most walls are higher than the average person can reach, and you need a means of getting to the top of them. A pair of ordinary household steps is all you need for this. A scaffold board is no use when you are hanging paper on a wall.

Plumbline and Bob

The paper must be hung truly vertical, and to ensure this you will need a plumbline and bob. Purpose-built versions are available but this is one item you would be justified in improvizing – by tying a small weight (anything you like – a nut for instance) on to a length of string. An old typewriter ribbon spool is a good thing to keep your makeshift plumbline on, and it helps you to use the line properly, as I will explain later on in this section.

Paperhanging Brush

There are two tools used for smoothing the paper to the wall. Firstly you brush it in place, using a proper paperhanger's brush, and here you cannot make do with a paintbrush instead. One possible makeshift favoured by many do-it-yourselfers is a clothesbrush, but I feel you do not work so quickly or effectively with this. Your paperhanging brush must have soft bristles, especially if you are hanging embossed papers, because you use a dabbing motion to press the paper in place, and hard bristles might damage it.

Seam Roller

The other tool is a seam roller. This is a small wooden or plastic roller with a small handle which, as its name implies, flattens down the join between two lengths of paper. There are two basic designs of seam roller. One has a fork-like handle that holds the roller between two prongs. In the other type, the roller is fixed to a single arm. This type is the most versatile, since you can get into corners with it.

Sponge or Rag

Lastly a sponge or old rag is always a handy thing to have around when you are hanging wallpaper, so that you can mop up splashes and the like.

What to Wear

A word about clothes. We all like to put on something old when we are doing jobs around the house, and do-it-yourselfers don a variety of old jeans, overalls and boiler suits. This is fine when you are painting, but when you are wallpapering you constantly need to lay your hands on a wide variety of tools, and you will speed up your work if these are readily accessible. The decorator likes to have an apron with a pocket, kangaroo-like, at the front, in which he can put his tape, pencil, scissors, paperhanging brush, seam roller etc., so that he can find them the minute he wants them. You may already have a gardening apron, used for a similar purpose.

Order of Work

If you are going to paper the walls of a room, then any

painting of woodwork etc. should be done first. Not only will this cut out the risk of splashing newly hung paper, but it will save the bother of cutting in where such stretches of woodwork as the door and window frames, skirtings, etc. meet the plaster. As you paint these items you can let the paint stray on to the wall as it will, knowing that you will later hide it with your wallcovering.

If you are papering the ceiling, this should be done before the walls. Many do-it-yourself decorators prefer to treat the ceiling with emulsion instead. Obviously the ceiling should be painted before the walls are papered. But don't be put off papering a ceiling. I hope to convince you that it is not difficult, on page 113.

→ **Where in the room should you start your wallpapering? It all depends on what sort of pattern you have chosen. A paper with a small, unobtrusive pattern, a plain texture, or a vertical stripe is the easiest thing to hang. With this kind you begin in a corner near the window and work towards the door. When you get to the door go back to the other window corner, and once again work towards the door.**

There are two reasons for this sequence. In the first place, if you are working away from the light, joins between the various drops will be less likely to show. Secondly the perimeter of your room will not be equivalent to an exact number of rolls, and you have to lose a fraction of a width somewhere. A favourite place for this is over the door.

→ **Much harder to handle are papers with a large, dominant pattern, for, in the jargon of the trade, they have to be 'set out' properly, otherwise they look ridiculous. So with them you should begin on a dominant architectural feature, which in many rooms is the chimney breast.**

Find the centre of the chimney breast and work

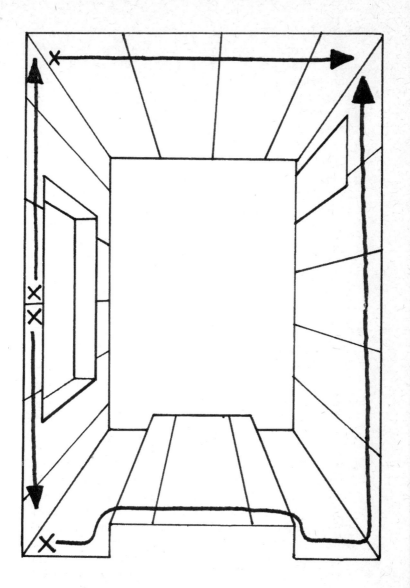

Fig. 17 Wallpapering: order of work

outwards from there. Some patterns will look better with the first roll centred on this line, others with a length hung both sides of it. There is one easy way to find out and that is to stick three or four shallow strips of the paper actually in position, and decide which looks best. Having finished the face of the chimney breast, you must turn your attention to the fireplace alcoves if you have them; once again set the paper out centrally, leaving half rolls, if need be, on the sides of the chimney breast.

In a room without a chimney breast you would probably take, as the dominant architectural feature, the wall at which everyone looks when sitting down to relax.

As you work your way around the room, bear in mind the importance of balancing a paper of this sort, and set it out properly. Considerable craftsmanship is called for in coping with a large pattern, and I would strongly advise that you cut your teeth with a simple pattern. Eventually, however, you will gain confidence and experience and you can go on to tackle more ambitious jobs.

Mixing the Paste

Your first job should be to mix your paste. Most wallcovering adhesives have to stand for a while after they have been added to water, and you can get on with cutting up the rolls into the correct lengths while you wait the requisite fifteen minutes or so.

Be sure, incidentally, to specify the right glue. You will never produce a good job if the one you are using is not strong enough, or is unsuitable in some other way. In general you must use a cellulose adhesive for ordinary lightweight papers, a starch-based one for heavier-duty papers, and one with a fungicide for vinyls because the glue cannot 'breathe' through the plastic facing of these coverings, and mould would grow underneath. But always check whenever you buy a paper what type of glue the manufacturer recommends. After all, if you follow his instructions, and things go wrong, you have a sound basis for complaint. But if you find the paper coming away from the wall and you have used a different kind of paste, the manufacturer cannot be held to blame.

Many professionals fix lengths of string across their bucket – they tie the string to the handle holders – to form a brush rest. If you leave the brush standing up in the paste, it will flop down into it, and glue will get all over the handle. If you rest it on any old surface it might pick up dust and dirt, or drop glue on the floor, which could then become slippery. So this is a tip well worth adopting.

Follow closely the instructions on the packet when mixing the glue. Normally you pour into the bucket the correct amount of water (the professional is so used to doing this that he can judge with his eye just how much to use, but you would do better to use a measuring jug), then sprinkle in the paste slowly and gradually, stirring it with a clean stick as you do so. Be careful not to pour the powder too quickly, otherwise lumps tend to form.

If in doubt, you should always mix your paste too thick, rather than too thin. It is easy to thin down thick paste by adding extra water to it, but you can't add extra powder to thin paste, because it will just go lumpy.

Now put the bucket safely on one side where it will not get kicked over while you get on with other things.

If you are at all worried about whether you have mixed the paste to the right strength or not, you can make a simple test. Load your brush with paste, and dab it on the back of a length of paper you are to hang. Now lift the brush; if the paper comes with it, the paste is all right.

Mix right at the start enough paste to do the whole job. It will not go off, even if it has to be left overnight.

When you are tackling only a small job you will want to use only a half, or perhaps a quarter, of the packet. Divide it up by weight, using the kitchen scales. Then write on the packet what proportion is left.

Measuring Up

Measure the height of the wall to be covered from the top of the skirting board to the picture rail if there is one, otherwise to the ceiling. Then add 75 mm (3 ins) as a trimming allowance – ie 38 mm (1½ ins) top and bottom – and that is the length to which you should cut each drop.

The measurement obviously has to be transferred to the paper. You can do this by placing your rule on an unrolled length, and marking it. Far better and quicker, however, to have a calibrated pasting table, so that as you unroll the paper you see at a glance where you must cut. Calibrating a table is easy enough. Get a 2-m (6-ft plus) dressmaker's tape, cut it to length and glue it to the top of your table.

Alternatively you can paint measurements on your table, using some dark (black is the best colour) leftover paint. Do not think that such a job would be beyond your capabilities – you are not working to very high standards of accuracy in cutting wallpaper to length. You need an artist's brush – one borrowed from your child's box of paints would be just the thing – and with it make a series of thin marks. The rule you create this way need not be very detailed. A longish mark could denote every 200 mm say, or each foot if you are still working in imperial measures. Then a mark half its length can go in between, then finally a shorter one halfway between that. Thus, in metric you would have marked every 50 mm, in imperial every 3 in. That should be quite enough detail for you to work.

Whatever type of calibration you decide on, you will find it easier to work if the rule is on the near side of the table.

It is necessary, incidentally, to measure only the first drop you cut for each wall. All subsequent ones are cut to the same length, using this first drop as a guide.

Sizing

The walls need to be sized before you can hang paper on them, because they would otherwise be too absorbent and would dry up the adhesive on the back of the paper too quickly. This means that the paper would not stick so well and you would not get so much 'slip' as you tried to slide it into position. You can buy special size, but the adhesive you are using on the paper will do. There should be instructions on the back of the packet telling you how to mix the powder to use it as size. Apply the size to the wall with your pasting brush. Take care that you spread the size out evenly, and that you cover the entire surface.

Shading the Rolls

Look on the back of the roll, where you will find a number. Check that all the numbers on each roll are exactly the same. These are known as batch numbers, and papers that have ostensibly the same pattern in an identical colourway can show slight variations in shades if they were not printed at the same time – in other words if they are not part of the same batch. These variations will not be very marked, and you will notice them only if lengths from different batches are hung side by side. So if you find among your rolls papers from a different batch make sure they do not go on the same wall. If doing so would leave you with a lot of waste paper, go back to the shop – before you have cut the rolls up, of course – and explain what has happened. The shop ought to change them for you.

Finally, partly unwind all the rolls of paper you have bought, and place them one on top of each other on your table to check visually that they all match up properly – a process that the tradesman calls 'shading before hanging'.

Cutting to Length

Once you are sure that everything is all right you can start to cut the paper to length.

Don't just unwind the paper and cut it to length haphazardly. First determine which is the top of the pattern, so that you do not hang it upside down. Nothing looks so ridiculous and amateurish as that, yet it can easily happen if you don't watch out. Wallpaper is wound and re-wound so often during manufacture that you cannot assume that the bit that comes off the roll first is the top.

Next you must remember that it is the pattern at the top of the wall that will be noticed by people entering the room, and it has to start at a sensible place where it will look attractive and not comical. **So find such a spot as near to the beginning of the roll as possible, where, in the words of the decorator, the pattern is full, then add your 38 mm (1½ ins) trimming allowance and cut the paper there. There will be a small amount of waste at the start of the roll.**

Having cut the paper at the top, cut it to its proper length, which is the height of the wall, plus another trimming allowance of 38 mm (1½ ins). In other words, it will be 75 mm (3 ins) larger than the wall it has to cover. Take great care over this first drop, for you use it as a guide for cutting the rest. The tradesman cuts at one go all the paper he will need for one wall, except perhaps for a few short bits. But it is not enough that all subsequent drops should equal the first one in length – they should also all start at the same point in the pattern repeat, so that they will match up exactly on the wall.

Pasting the Paper

Pasting tables are usually about 1·8 m (6 ft) long and 55 cm (22 ins wide). In other words they are not as long as most of your drops of paper will be, but they are slightly wider. Place your paper on the table. If it will not lie flat, back-roll it to ensure that it does so. When you start to paste, the top of the paper should be positioned to line up with the right-hand end, the bottom portion overhanging at the left. Next push the paper away from you so that its far edge slightly overhangs the back edge of the table. Now you can begin pasting.

To charge the brush, dip it into the paste so that its bristles are submerged for about two-thirds of their depth, then press it against each side of the bucket in turn to make sure that the paste is evenly distributed and all excess has been squeezed out.

**Mentally divide that part of the paper on the table- ←
top into quarters, and paste them in the order shown. Apply the paste with your right hand and hold the paper steady with the left.** Thus you will be able to

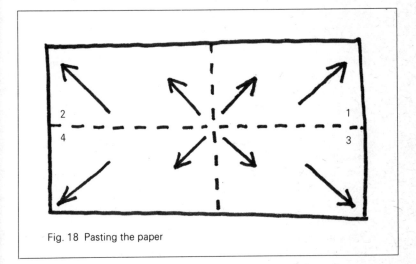

Fig. 18 Pasting the paper

ensure that your left hand is always on a dry bit of paper. If you put your left hand on a pasted portion of paper you will get your fingertip wet, which can be a downright nuisance and a source of real irritation. But that's not all. You will be drying off the paper at that point and it is not unknown for five little blobs to show through when a paper has been hung and finally dried out – especially on the ceiling – precisely because the decorator put his hand on a pasted portion of the paper.

Paste with a series of zigzag strokes from the centre of the paper towards the edge. If you do the opposite – ie paste from the edge of the paper inwards – you would undoubtedly get paste on the face of the paper.

After you have pasted the two far quarters, drag the paper towards you (make sure you don't get hold of a pasted portion), allowing it this time to overhang slightly the nearside edge. Now finish pasting the last two quarters. To speed things up, the professional never once during this whole process puts his brush down to rest, for he would waste time and effort stooping down to pick it up again.

With all four quarters pasted, take hold of the right-hand edge of the paper, each corner between a thumb and middle finger. Raise it and move it to the far end of the table, letting it drop gently so that the paper is neatly and squarely folded in two, the edges parallel, top to bottom. To make sure that you will not get any paste on the ceiling when you come to hang the paper, fold over the top 19 mm ($\frac{3}{4}$ in.) ie about half the extra bit that you allowed for trimming.

Move the folded paper along to the right, and in the case of paper cut to fit a room of normal height you should now be able to accommodate the rest of it on your table. Again, this will need back-rolling if it starts to curl up. Paste as already described, then take hold of it at the left-hand end and fold inwards until its edge meets that of the previous fold. If any paste gets on to the table-top during this process sponge it off immediately, for cleanliness is all-important when you are hanging wallpaper.

Your paper has now been properly pasted and folded. It should have one large fold (the top one) and a smaller one at the bottom – the proportions will probably be about two-thirds to one-third.

If you are dealing with an embossed or duplex paper (ie

one that consists of two layers of paper bonded together) it needs to be left to soak. Simplex (single-layer) papers do not need soaking. One of the snags of soaking wallpaper, however, is that if you leave it saturated it will stretch. To be able to match up the patterns you have to make sure that each length of paper stretches by exactly the same amount. There is only one way to ensure that – leave each of them to soak for exactly the same length of time. Somewhere between 10 and 15 minutes is ideal. The professional is able to judge this by instinct – in any case he can tell when the paper is ready for hanging because it will feel soft and supple. But for you it would be a good idea to write in pencil on the back of the paper, at the top where it will get trimmed off, the time at which you finished pasting. Then you will know when you can start to hang the paper.

At first you will sit around waiting for 10 minutes to pass between pasting and hanging, but as you become more experienced you will do as the tradesman does – paste two, hang two. In fact, the best tradesmen would paste three and hang three, but I doubt whether a do-it-yourselfer would ever do enough decorating to become so proficient.

Dropping a Plumbline

Make sure that your first length of paper is hung truly vertical, for its position will determine that of all the others on the wall. You do this by dropping a plumbline.

Let us assume that you are starting at the left-hand end of a wall, and working towards the right. Reverse all the following instructions if you are working from right to left. Place your steps there, climb them and at the top of the wall, at ceiling level, make a pencil mark – the width of a roll of wallpaper less 12 mm ($\frac{1}{2}$ in.) from the left-hand end. There is no need to take any measurements for this. Just place a spare roll of paper on the wall to act as a gauge. Hold the top of your plumbline on this pencil mark.

→ If you have adopted the trick on page 82 of wrapping the line round an old typewriter spool, hold the spool in the palm of your hand, which you can press hard against the wall, letting the string pass over your thumb, so that the weight can swing freely. In any event, let it do so until it stops swinging – you can steady it by jamming a knee up against it, but don't force it into an 'untrue' position. Make sure your thumb is holding the line on the pencil mark. When the line is steady, make a mark along it on the wall with a pencil held in the other hand. Start this line fairly near to the top of the wall – certainly within 150 mm (6 ins) – and continue it downwards for as long as you comfortably can. It would be impossible for you to draw from top to bottom of the wall, and in any event there is no need to do so. Incidentally, you must make sure that your pencil line is directly behind the line – many do-it-yourselfers are misled into drawing on the line's shadow.

Hanging the Paper

Take your pasted paper and put it neatly over one arm. Then climb your steps. Take hold of the paper with each corner edge of the top between the thumb and finger of one hand. The small portion that you folded over at the top will, as well as keeping paste off the ceiling, ensure that your fingers stay dry. As you hold the paper, let it
→ fall out of its top fold. **So that it will not go crashing down too much, however, stretch out one foot, balancing yourself on the other, and hold the bottom fold on the outstretched instep.**

Bring the paper to the wall, place the top right-hand edge on the plaster and, with your hand flat on top of this, slide this edge into the correct position. It is important not to place the whole width of the paper flat on the wall as you do this sliding – you would never move it; just one small portion is sufficient. And what is your aim in this sliding? Two things. Firstly, you want to ensure that the break in the pattern where the top meets the ceiling comes in an attractive and logical position, as explained in the section on cutting. Take great care over this with the first drop. Its position will determine that of all the others. Secondly, you must make sure that the drop is truly vertical. Adjust its right hand edge so that it just 'kisses' the pencil line you have made with the aid of your plumbline. Take very great care with this first length.

When you are satisfied with the positioning you can let the paper lie flat on the wall, and use your paperhanging brush to smooth it into place. Work from the centre of the paper outwards, smoothing it nicely into place. Use not-too-heavy strokes for this, so that you do not alter the positioning of the paper. In particular, be sure not to move it from the vertical. Brush it well into the angle where it meets the ceiling, using a dabbing motion.

You will note that the paper goes 12 mm ($\frac{1}{2}$ in.) or so on the adjacent wall, all the way down its length. This is correct, because this turn will be covered when you come to paper that wall.

Now you can trim the paper where it meets the ceiling. Take your closed scissors and draw the back of the point along the meeting line between wall and ceiling so that they lightly score the paper. Peel the paper away from the wall and, working from the reverse side, cut along the score line neatly and cleanly. Sponge off any paste that has got on to the ceiling, then brush the paper back into place. Now pull the paper out of its bottom fold and smooth it in place. **The technique of marking for** ⟵ **trimming it to fit the skirting is slightly different, because you use a pencil. Hold the pencil upright, and almost flat against the wall, then draw it along the paper where it touches the skirting board. The line will be slightly away from the wall.** Peel the paper away, and working from its face side cut the paper just inside (ie above) the line, which will ensure a good fit and also that no pencil mark will be visible on the finished work. Then brush the paper back in place. If any paste gets on to the skirting board, wipe it off with your rag or sponge.

The pencil gives a better and much more accurate line to which to cut. Why don't we use this method at the top? Because with a pencil line, you have to cut on the face side of the paper, and at the top that would involve almost standing on your head, or pulling too much of the paper away to allow you to see the decorative side.

Subsequent lengths of paper are hung in much the same way. However, with these you bring the top *left*-hand edge of the paper to the wall first, and slide it into position so that you get a good pattern match with the first drop, then smooth this into place. Top and bottom trimming is done just as for the first drop.

You do not need a plumbline for this second drop, because you are butting it up to the first one.

Using the Seam Roller

Now – except on an embossed paper, where you should never use it – it is time to bring the seam roller into play. It is essential to use this tool on vinyl. The purpose of a seam roller is to flatten the join between the two lengths and stick it down firmly, but you have to be careful using it because you may just end up polishing a thin strip each side of the join, which will show up as a shiny length in the finished job. This is what you have to do. **The seam roller tapers slightly at the end furthest from the single arm, and it is just this tapered tip that comes into contact with the paper. The taper means that you could not accurately bring the roller right down the join in one long movement, and instead you must make a series of strokes in a zigzag motion. But don't make too many strokes, otherwise you will get the polished effect.**

Now carry on hanging the third and subsequent drops.

The End of the Wall

Eventually you will come to the end of the wall, and, inevitably, the last drop will need to be narrower than the roll of paper. Because the walls of a house are never true, this last drop will not be a uniform width all down its length. Measure it at its widest point – if you stand back you will normally be able to see where this is, but if you can't, take measurements at random points to find it.

To the widest measurement add 12 mm ($\frac{1}{2}$ in.) and cut your roll to this width. Here's how you do that. **Place it ←︎ pattern-upwards on your pasting table, lay your rule on the face of the paper and mark the required width**

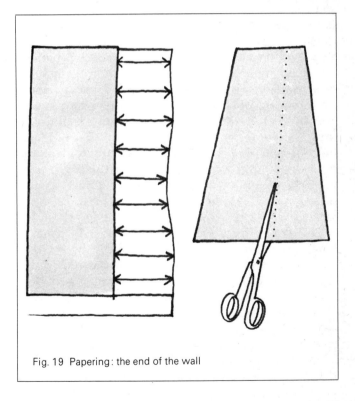

Fig. 19 Papering: the end of the wall

at intervals of 300 mm (12 ins) or so all along the length of the paper. Now stand at one end of the table, sight along the pencil marks and cut to them with your scissors. You will find that this method works perfectly – there is no need to join up the marks with a pencil line.

You will now have two lengths of paper: one cut to width, which we will call piece A, and the other portion, which we will call B. Do not throw this away.

Paste, hang and trim piece A in the normal way, turning it round the corner by its small surplus width as needed.

On the return wall drop and mark a plumbline the width of piece B from the corner. Paste piece B and hang it to this plumbline. It will overlap piece A by varying amounts, according to how far out of true the walls are. **You will find it impossible to get a good pattern match down the whole drop, so you should aim to do your perfect matching at the eye level of a person standing up, because that will be the most obvious part of the join, and the one that people will notice most when they enter the room. The top and bottom matching will have to work out as it comes.**

Now you can complete the rest of the wall in the normal way, butting up the first complete length against piece B, and following on with subsequent drops in the same way.

The above is the method for dealing with what is known as an internal angle – ie one in which the return wall comes towards you. However, you also come across external angles – where the wall at the corner goes away from you. The most obvious instance of this is at the ends of a chimney breast. But you can come across external angles in other parts of the room, wherever there are recesses other than chimney breast alcoves.

External angles are much easier to deal with, because normally you can take the paper right round

them. However, where the angle is a long way from being truly upright, there can be problems, and it is then better to turn the corner with two drops, by cutting the paper into two pieces in a similar manner to that described for an internal corner.

Piece A on the face of the chimney breast (assuming that it is a chimney breast we are tackling) should be about 25 mm (1 in.) or so greater than the widest point of the drop, and should be hung first, leaving the excess width sticking out. Hang piece B on the return wall to a plumbline in the normal way, trying to match up the pattern. Now brush the excess of piece A round the corner and on top of piece B so that the raw edge of piece B will not be visible from the middle of the room. You might have to smear a little extra paste underneath the edge of piece A to get it to stick.

Dealing with Light Switches

There are two basic types of light switch: the modern kind, which are rectangular and fit fairly flush to the wall; and the old-fashioned types that are circular and stand proud of the wall.

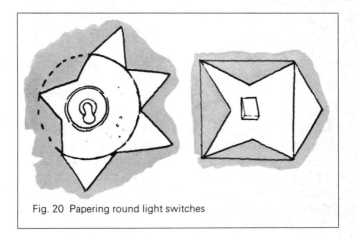

Fig. 20 Papering round light switches

The former is by now probably the more common, so let us deal with it first. Hang your length of paper, making sure that its pattern matches up with that of the adjacent drop, and allowing it to lie on top of the switch. **Spear the paper at the centre of the switch with the point of your closed scissors, and from this hole make a scissor-cut to each of the four corners of the switch. You will be left with four flaps. Fold these back, mark with a pencil where they touch the edge of the switch just as you would when trimming the paper to the skirting board, and cut along this line.** It is permissible to hide any 'tails' under the cover of the switch (always providing that you are not dealing with a metallic paper – see page 77). Pull the switch cover away from the wall by withdrawing the screws you see on its face, having first turned off the electricity at the mains, and push the 'tails' underneath. Then screw the cover down again and restore the power.

The principle of dealing with a round switch is similar, in that you spear the paper at the centre of the switch in just the same way. However, you make many more cuts from the centre outwards, until you are left with a lot of little tails. Brush these well into the base of the switch, and mark them where they touch it. Then you can trim them to fit neatly, and brush them well back into place.

In both cases you will need to lift the paper away from the wall to do the cutting.

Trimming Round a Doorway

At least one wall of the room will have a doorway, and one drop of paper will need to be cut to a sort of L-shape to fit round it. Here's how you do that.

Hang the drop in the normal way, matching it up to the adjacent drop at one side, and letting it lie over the face of the door frame, with the door closed, at the other.

Make a diagonal scissor-cut from the outer edge of ←
the paper to the top outside point of the door frame.
It will now be possible to brush the paper down flat,
with waste sticking up all round the door frame. Trim
the paper first to meet the ceiling, in the normal way.
Then trim it to fit the top and side of the door opening,
using the pencil-marking method described for cutting to
the skirting board on page 91. Finally, cut it to fit the
skirting.

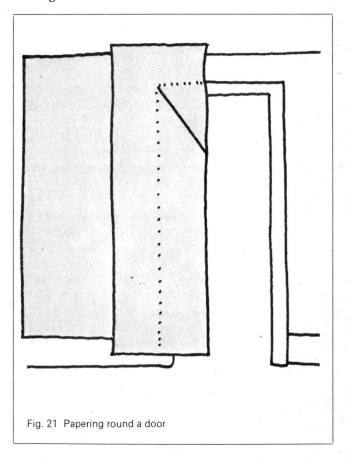

Fig. 21 Papering round a door

In modern small homes, doorways are usually right at the end of a wall, so all you now have to do to complete that particular wall is hang a short, narrow piece over the opening. This, as explained on page 80, is a good place to 'lose' a half-width drop. However, it may be that you will need a second L-shaped piece, cut in just the same way, at the other side of the door. This second L-shaped piece could be narrow, to allow you to 'lose' the half width. In the case of very wide door openings – french windows, for instance, or intercommunicating doors between a living and dining room – you will need an L-shaped piece at each end, as well as several short drops between.

Coping with Fireplaces

A simple uncomplicated modern fireplace is dealt with just like a wide door opening – ie you will need an L-shaped piece at each end, and shorter drops in the middle. But, of course, since a chimney breast is the most instantly obvious part of the room, you must not try to 'lose' narrow drops here.

In Victorian or older houses, however, you may have a fireplace with a lot of ornate moulding at each end. The way of dealing with this is similar to the method for tackling a round light switch – ie you make a lot of short cuts away from the moulding, then brush the paper back in place, leaving a lot of tails sticking up. Mark these with a pencil where they meet the moulding, pull them back and cut them to fit. The more complicated the moulding, the more cuts (and tails) you will have to make to fit.

Finally, brush the tails back in place, and they will not be noticeable.

The Window Wall

Since you start papering a room in the angles at each end of the window wall and work towards the door (see page

80), the window wall itself is something that has to be tackled in isolation, and it is best if you make it the last job in the room. Some older houses have a complete wooden frame round the window opening, and you deal with this as though it were a doorway, cutting in under the bottom of the frame in the same way as you did at the top. More tricky, however, is the arrangement found in most modern homes where there is an opening – known in trade jargon as a reveal – in which the window is set. This is the procedure for dealing with a wall in which there is a reveal.

First find the centre point of the wall over the window, and drop and mark a plumbline there. Begin hanging short drops of paper from the ceiling, carrying them

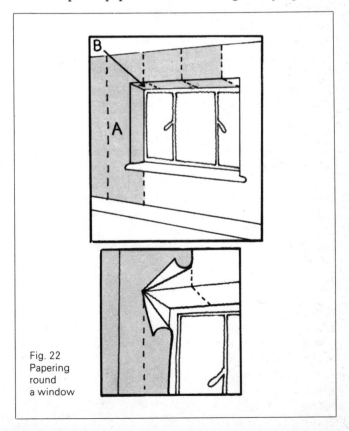

Fig. 22
Papering
round
a window

under the top of the reveal – or soffit, as this top is known – to meet the timber of the window frame itself. Your first of these short drops can be centred on the plumbline or just to the side of it; work out which arrangement will give you the best turn into the side of the window – you will see what this means as we carry on with the instructions.

Trim the short drops in the usual way to the ceiling and frame. Normally, you can go straight from ceiling to frame with one length, but if the angle is badly out of true it might be better to do this with two pieces – ie first cover the soffit with a small piece of paper, then paper the wall over the opening from ceiling to soffit. This top piece would overlap that on the soffit – since the overlap would be pointing away from the room, it would not be visible.

Carry on hanging short drops on one side of the first – you can work to the left or right just as you wish, but for the rest of these instructions I will assume that you are working to the left.

Eventually, you will come to the point where you have to deal with your first floor-to-ceiling drop – let us call this piece A in the diagram. It will, of course, butt up to the short drop on its right, but even so it is an aid to greater accuracy if you also drop a plumbline on its left, and hang it to this.

Brush the paper in place until it lies over the window opening. Now make two horizontal cuts – one along the line of the soffit, the other along the line of the window ledge. You will be left with a sort of hinge that you can turn down the side of the opening. It is better if this hinge stretches to the frame, and you can usually arrange this according to the positioning of the first short drop over the top of the window, in relation to the plumbline. Otherwise, you will have to fill in with a narrow strip. Brush the hinge against the side of the reveal, mark with a pencil its meeting line with the frame, peel it back and cut it, then smooth it down. The drop should now be trimmed round any projecting window ledge and in the normal way to the ceiling and skirting.

There will still be a small part of the soffit, at its far left end, to be covered. Do this with a small, separate piece of paper (piece B in the diagram), which you match up to the rest of the paper on the soffit. Piece B must pass over the edge of the soffit, and pass up and under piece A at this point – you will have to peel piece A away from the wall to allow it to do this, then brush it back in place.

Now go back to the top of the window and work to the right in just the same way. Finish off by hanging short drops under the window ledge.

Some windows go right up to the ceiling, in which case you begin your papering with a full-length drop on each side of it, cutting the drops just at sill level to turn into the reveal. You might then be left with a half-width drop under the window, but this would not matter too much, especially if the wall there is not very high, and you intend to put furniture in front of it. Your problems are least of all where there is a floor-to-ceiling window with no wall underneath to be papered.

With the area around the window completed, you can now carry on hanging drops in the normal way right to the ends of the wall. At each end you are certain to need a drop that is less than full width, and you measure for this and cut it as described in the section on completing the end of a wall (page 93).

Do you remember how when you started out from these corners you allowed a small overlap to go on the window wall (page 91)? Your last drops here will overlap this to ensure a very neat job. Once again aim to get your best pattern match at the eye level of a person standing.

Papering a window wall is not all that difficult. But if you still think it's too much for you, here's a tip. Just paper up to the edge of the opening, and paint the walls of the reveal in the same paint as that on the window frames and ledge. No one will notice what you have done.

Papering a Stairwell

There are two problems about papering a stairwell. The first is actually getting up to those high spots, which involves complicated scaffolding. The second is that you will be hanging side by side widely differing lengths of paper. That means they will also vary in weight when wet, and the longer lengths of paper will stretch more than their neighbouring short ones. That is going to cause you real problems in matching up the patterns. And that's something that takes real craftsmanship, and years of experience, to overcome. So in the meantime, while you are still a beginner, it is best to avoid papers with a strong horizontal pattern match in this situation. Papers with vertical stripes would be your best bet, but there are other patterns where the matching is not all that important.

The Waste Bits

The result of all the trimming will be a lot of left-over bits and pieces of paper. What are you to do with them? One thing you must not do is simply throw them on the ground to lie around anywhere, for wet paste is slippery and you could have a nasty accident as a result of standing on a piece of paper. So you must carefully put them somewhere out of harm's way. The traditional place for this was the fireplace (with the fire unlit, of course) because that is somewhere you would not want to walk, and yet the paper would not be piled up against a wall needing to be decorated. Today, of course, many rooms do not have a fireplace. The best alternative is a plastic sack or other receptacle. Then when the job is done you simply dispose of the sackful of paper.

Hanging Vinyl Wallcoverings

You hang a vinyl wallcovering in pretty much the same

way you deal with ordinary wallcoverings, but there are one or two differences. You must, of course, use a suitable adhesive (see page 86). Vinyls need one that has a fungicide, as explained earlier. And the only size you can use is one made from this special adhesive. There is no need to allow vinyl to soak once you have pasted it.

You can use a Stanley knife with a sharp blade to ← **trim a vinyl at skirting level. Place a straight edge on the paper where it meets the skirting, then run your knife along it to cut it to fit; it is much quicker than the pencil and scissors method needed for trimming wallpaper (page 96). This will not, however, work with ordinary wallpaper, for you cannot cut wet wallpaper cleanly with a knife – it tears and you get a ragged line.** Where the angle between ceiling and wall is true you can use the knife and straight edge method on vinyl here, too. More often than not, however, the line will wiggle all over the place, and you will have to use the scissors method described for cutting wallpaper at ceiling level (page 95).

Another big problem with vinyls is that, using the normal vinyl paste, you cannot stick vinyl on top of vinyl – something that is necessary at, for instance, corners (page 97). You may get away with a small overlap, and one thing you can do is leave it in position for a day or two in the hope that it will stick. If it does not, you can always re-stick the join neatly, using a latex adhesive such as Copydex.

There is another dodge, however, and one that ← **you should use where you get a large overlap. Smooth the second length down in place so that it overlaps the first. Now make a vertical knife cut through the centre of the overlap, using a straight edge or the pattern of the paper as a guide. The blade of the knife must be really sharp, otherwise it will tear the paper instead of cutting it. Open up the joint and you will be left with two long, thin, separated**

strips of vinyl. Peel these off and throw them away. Smooth the remaining vinyl in place, go over the join with a seam roller, and you will get a perfect join and very neat finish.

Ready-pasteds

Some wallcoverings (most of them vinyls, but some papers, too) do not need to be pasted, because they are self-adhesive. They are known as ready-pasteds. It is impossible for me to give you any tradesman's tricks for handling these papers, because by and large he doesn't use them. They cost too much.

Direct price comparisons between ordinary papers and ready-pasteds are impossible to make, because a particular pattern comes either with or without paste. There is no choice. You cannot look at a pattern and decide in which version you would like to buy it. However, ready-pasted paper has obvious attractions for the do-it-yourselfer, so let me tell you how to use it, and give one or two tips that might help you make more of it.

Ready-pasted paper is treated on the back with a coating of adhesive, but this adhesive needs to be soaked in water to become activated. When you buy a ready-pasted paper, you are given a cardboard trough which you fill with water up to the recommended level. Watch this level as you work, by the way, for the water will need topping up from time to time. Place the tray on the floor under the length of wall that the first drop will cover.

Cut the first drop to length, allowing the normal trimming allowance top and bottom, then roll it up and soak it in the trough for the time the manufacturer recommends. It is important that you follow this recommendation exactly. Too much immersion in water, and you might wash the glue off, and anyway the paper will become too soft and tear easily. Too little, and the glue will not work properly. However, it is better to be, say, half a minute over rather than half a minute under time. If it is a paper you are dealing with, you *must* roll it with the pattern inside; with a vinyl you can have the pattern inside or out. In both cases it is vital for the roll to be only loosely wound so that water can get at every part of the adhesive. The other important point is that you should start rolling the paper from the bottom, so that the top of the pattern will be on the outside of the finished roll, and it will be the top that you first draw out of the trough.

After the recommended soaking period draw the roll out, unwinding it as you do so, and immediately hang it on the wall. The normal rules about sliding it into position, matching up the pattern, and trimming it to fit all apply. However, while you are working on the top part of the paper, leave the bottom hanging over the trough, so that any excess water will run over the surface of the wallcovering – especially if it is a vinyl – and go safely into the trough, instead of on your floor. Even so, you might want to place a small sheet of polythene or something similar under the trough to guard against splashes.

When you come to work on the bottom of the length, move the tray along so that it is in the correct position for the next drop, and put this in to soak now so that it will be ready when you come to work on it.

When smoothing the wallcovering down in place, it is best to use a sponge for vinyls and flat unembossed papers, but for heavy embossed papers use a paperhanging brush.

Where you have a very long drop (the most usual place is the staircase) the technique of soaking needs to be slightly different, because with the normal method the moisture would not get at the heart of the roll.

This is what you must do. Roll the paper loosely with the pattern inside, but this time starting from the top of the drop so that the bottom of the pattern will be at the end of the roll when you have finished. Dunk the roll in the trough. Now, with the paper still submerged in the trough, rewind it, but this time as tightly as possible. To avoid any strain on your back when you bend down to do this, place the trough on a table at a convenient height for working. However, on no account must you try to minimize the discomfort of the cold water by using hot, because this will soften the paper too quickly, making it difficult to hang, and will cause lack of adhesion.

Your winding will mean that the pattern is now on the outside, and the top of the drop is at the end – all very convenient for when you begin hanging. Pull the paper, still in a roll, out of the trough, gripping it lightly in the middle of the roll with the palm of one hand. Hold it vertically, first one way then the other, so that all the excess water drains out and into the trough. now you can hang it, holding the roll in one hand, matching the pattern with the other, and feeding it from the roll as you move down the wall.

You can see that such a roll of paper will be very rigid, and because of that ready-pasteds are much easier for the do-it-yourselfer to hang on a ceiling – as you will see when we get to the subject (page 113) it is the way that folded ceiling paper flops about that makes it difficult for the do-it-yourselfer to control.

How to Hang Lining Papers

Many people seem to shun lining papers – you have only to ask at your local shops about these papers to discover that. **Professionals, however, make extensive use of them – as a preliminary cover-up for walls that are in bad condition, and also to ensure a really tip-top finish for heavyweight and hand-printed papers.** Indeed, some of the really top-class professionals would never dream of hanging any sort of paper on any kind of surface without lining first, and if you want your work to look professional I would advise you to do the same. In fact, the only time when you can really dispense with a lining paper is when you are hanging a lightweight paper on a perfect surface. In addition, hanging lining papers is excellent practice for coping with a ceiling.

There are various grades of lining paper. The worse the condition of your wall, the thicker the lining you need. Linings are available, too, in light and dark shades. Always hang a dark lining under a dark top paper and vice versa, so that if your paper does open up a little at the joins, it will not be quite so noticeable. There are also lining papers suitable for taking paint.

Lining papers are always hung in the opposite direction to the paper that will cover them – hence the phrase 'cross lining' which the professional uses. On a wall, therefore, this means that the lining is hung horizontally. Some walls are in such a bad condition that it is a good idea to hang two lining papers on them. In such cases the first paper will be hung vertically just like wallpaper, and the second one horizontally in the normal lining paper manner. For a painted finish the lining is hung vertically, like ordinary paper. If you decide on two linings before painting, the first one should be horizontal.

The reason why the various layers go at right angles to each other is that paper which has been moistened by paste shrinks as it dries out, and this shrinkage is mainly across the width. The combined effect of the shrinkage of two papers hung in the same direction would tend to pull them apart at the joins, and that would look very unsightly indeed. In any event, even without such shrinkage, the fact that the two joins coincided would tend to produce an untidy effect.

Equipment

The equipment you need is exactly as for wallpapering, with one addition. Where the lining is to be hung horizontally, in most rooms a pair of steps will not be enough on their own when you are hanging the top length, as you need to walk at the right level all along the length of the wall. That means you need a scaffold board.

The lining paper should be cut to the same length as the wall, plus an allowance of about 38 mm ($1\frac{1}{2}$ ins) at each end for trimming.

Use an ordinary cellulose paste for lining papers, mixed according to the manufacturer's instructions. The lining is pasted in much the same way as ordinary wallpaper, but the folding is different. You need to fold the lining concertina-like with 230-mm (9-in.) pleats.

Cross Lining

When you hang lining paper there is no need for any pencilled guideline. If you are cross lining, aim to follow the line of the ceiling with the first length, leaving a 6-mm ($\frac{1}{4}$ in.) gap all the way round – ie between the top of the paper and the ceiling, and at each end. Pull out the first fold of paper and position it accurately on the wall, then brush it in place. Then let the next fold come out, position it accurately, and brush it in place. Walk along letting the paper unwind from its folds, and brush it accurately into place as you go. When the whole length has been hung, walk along it smoothing it out with your brush, from the centre of the paper outwards to the edges, to make sure there are no air bubbles trapped in the middle. Then trim it to length at the ends.

Now you can hang the second length in the same way, although in most rooms you will not have to stand on a scaffold board to do this. Once again, it is better to leave a 6-mm ($\frac{1}{4}$ in.) gap all round – ie between the two lengths of paper, as well as the ends. However, you can if you wish butt the two lengths up to each other, but under no circumstances should you allow them to overlap. If you find your second roll straying on to the first, then pull it down, re-position it accurately, and begin again.

Carry on with subsequent lengths in this way, until you have to cut one to width to fit the space available. Do this exactly as you cut the wallpaper to turn round a corner (page 93) – ie measure the gap to be filled every 300 mm (12 ins) or so, remembering to leave a 6-mm ($\frac{1}{4}$-in.) gap between the bottom of the paper and the skirting board, and transfer your reading to the paper, making a mark with a pencil. Then cut along the length of paper, to join up the marks. Paste and hang it in the normal way.

Hanging Lining Paper Vertically

Lining paper that is to be hung vertically can be treated just like wallpaper. The job is, however, much easier. There is no need to bother about a plumbline and you can follow the angle of the wall, leaving a gap of 6 mm ($\frac{1}{4}$ in.) between the first length and the corner. A similar gap should be left between the rolls and at the top and bottom. There is, of course, no pattern to match up, so there is no need to slide the paper around, and you do not need to leave so much trimming allowance at top and bottom.

Vertical lining paper that is to receive a painted finish should be butt jointed, otherwise the gap would show, and it should overlap at the corners of the room just like wallpaper.

Papering a Ceiling

If you go into the homes of most people who do their own decorating you will see that, even though the walls of a room may have been papered, in most cases the ceiling is treated with emulsion paint. The reason is obvious – preparing a ceiling is a job that terrifies most amateur decorators. But really you *can* manage it, provided you follow the instructions step-by-step. Let us see what is involved.

Incidentally, although I am dealing with it at the end of this section on wallpapering, ceiling paper should in fact be hung first. I have described the hanging of wallpaper first because that is what you ought to tackle before even thinking of taking on a ceiling.

Equipment

First of all, the equipment you need: except that you also need a piece of chalk, it is the same as for hanging lining paper – in other words, as for wallpaper with the essential, repeat essential, addition of a scaffold board. You will undoubtedly have heard of people who have papered their bedroom ceiling by starting off standing on the bed, stepping on to the dressing table and finishing up on a chest of drawers. These are frequently also the people who have nasty accidents.

Your paper should be cut to the same length as the ceiling, plus an allowance at each end of about 50 mm (2 ins) for trimming.

Hanging the Paper

Ceiling paper should be hung parallel to the wall containing the window (or the main window if there is more than one). Begin at this wall and work away from it. You need a guideline on the ceiling to which to hang your first length, so that it will be true, but since the surface on which you are working is not vertical you cannot make this with a plumbline and bob, as you would when wallpapering a wall (see page 93). Therefore you must 'snap a chalk line'. Here's how you do it.

Rub some chalk on your length of string. Get someone to hold one end of the string hard on the ceiling at one end of the room, while you hold the other at the opposite side. Make sure that the string is held taut and close to the ceiling. Now pull it back like a bowstring, and let it go with a twang. It will make a perfectly straight chalk line on the ceiling.

The correct position for this line is the width of a roll of paper from the window wall, less 12 mm ($\frac{1}{2}$ in.) or so. The reason for this is that the paper should overlap on to the walls by that 12-mm ($\frac{1}{2}$-in.) allowance on every ledge. This overlap will eventually be covered up by the paper you hang on the wall, and you will get a perfect join.

114

It is vital that you stand directly underneath the chalk line in the case of the first length, and underneath the joins between the various lengths for subsequent ones. You cannot hang ceiling paper accurately unless you are right beneath the line to which you are working. So begin by positioning your scaffold board safely and securely on its supports directly under the chalk line.

For this first length, you must stand facing the window, and a right-handed person would work from right to left. For all the remaining lengths you will need to stand with your back to the window, for that is the only way you can work directly under the joins. Since you will still be working from right to left, this means that you will be papering from the opposite end of the room to that at which you started the first length.

Bear this fact in mind when pasting and folding the paper. For the first length you must begin pasting and folding at the end opposite to that on which you start for the rest, otherwise it will be 'upside down', if you can use such a phrase for paper going on a ceiling. A wide variety of papers can be used on a ceiling nowadays. Until recently only the traditional ceiling papers were used, which are still available even though they are not now so popular – the bubbled kind for instance. Some of these do not seem to have a pattern as such. Nevertheless they have a texture, and if this is the wrong way round it will be noticeable in the finished result. Nowadays it is quite common to put an ordinary wallpaper on the ceiling – sometimes the same one that is going on the walls – and here it is vital to get the patterns the same way round. **To avoid any mistake that will be embarrassingly obvious in the finished job, always mark the paper when you cut it to indicate which is the top, so that you will be able to paste and fold it the right way round.**

Ceiling papers are pasted just like wallpapers (page 90)

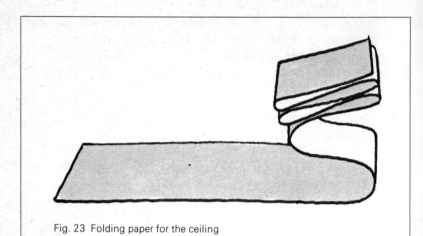

Fig. 23 Folding paper for the ceiling

but they are folded concertina-like, as for lining papers (page 112) but in 380- to 450-mm (15- to 18-in.) pleats.

→ **If you take hold of a length of pasted and folded ceiling paper you will find that it flops at each end like a pair of spaniel's ears. The way to stop that is to place a spare roll of paper underneath it as a support. That will hold it rigid.**

To hang the paper, climb up on your scaffold board, holding the roll of paper in your left hand. Unfold the first section of paper, place one edge on the ceiling, and slide it along with your right hand to position it accurately on the guideline. Then with your right hand take the paper-hanging brush out of your apron pocket and brush the paper in place, smoothing it out and making sure that you get rid of any air bubbles. Move along, allowing the next fold to open up, position that accurately on the guideline, and brush this in place. Carry on like this until the whole length has been hung.

116

The important thing is that you must keep your ←
left hand – the one holding the folded and pasted
paper – high up near the ceiling. Because this is a
tiring position to work in you will tend to let your
arm drop down to a more restful position. But if you
do you will find that you will be imposing too great a
strain on the paste, which will simply be unable to
hold the paper on the ceiling, and you will go on
brushing and brushing at paper that, infuriatingly,
keeps falling down.

When the complete length has been hung, walk along
your scaffold board giving the paper a final smooth, and
checking that no air bubbles have been trapped, then
trim it at the ends. Remember that it must overlap ←
down the end walls, as well as those at the sides, by
about 12 mm ($\frac{1}{2}$ in.). There is no need to measure this,
however. Use your forefinger as a guide.

Now you can paste and hang the next length (I assume
that you will not be up to 'pasting two and hanging two'
when it comes to ceilings). For this second length, your
scaffold board will remain in the same position, for since
it is directly under the chalk line, it will also be under the
far edge of the first length of paper, which is the guide to
which you will work when hanging the second length.
Position this second length so that it butts up against the
first, matching the pattern if there is one, then smooth it
in place with your brush. Hang the length all the way
along, just as you did the first, then trim it at the ends.

For the third roll you will need to move your scaffold
board along until it is under the far edge of the second
roll. Then you can hang this third piece of paper in the
same way that you dealt with the second one. Carry on in
this way until you come to the point where you have to
cut a width to fit the space remaining. This you do just as
when cutting wallpaper for the end of a wall (see page 97),
the only difference being that you do not keep the offcut,
for there is no corner round which to turn it. The cut edge

117

will be the one that overlaps the wall by 12 mm ($\frac{1}{2}$ in.) – just as the first length did – so it does not matter if your cutting is a little ragged, since it will be hidden by the paper on the wall.

One good thing about ceilings is that there are not so many obstructions as on a wall, so there is less fiddly cutting and trimming. One that you will meet, however, in just about every room is the rose for the ceiling light flex. If this comes in the middle of a length, tackle it as you would an old-fashioned round light switch (see page 99). Let the paper lie across the rose, marking where its centre meets the paper. Spear the paper there with your closed scissors, then make a series of star-shaped cuts outwards. Smooth the paper down in place all round the rose, then carry on hanging the length in the normal way. When you have finished the length, come back to the rose, where you will see a lot of little tails sticking up. Mark these with pencil where they meet the rose, then peel them back and cut them along the score line. Smooth them back in place, and your cutting will be completely disguised.

If the rose comes at the edge of a length, cut the tails from that edge inwards, then smooth them down and trim them.

Repairing a Ceiling in Bad Condition

Ceilings are often in a worse state of repair than walls. If the one you are tackling is bulging and falling away here and there, first go over it nailing it back to the joists, using galvanized clout nails. Clout nails are advisable because they have a big head, and would thus hold the ceiling more firmly in place; use galvanized ones so that they will not rust as they are dampened by the paste of the paper. Then hang lining paper first. Remember how I said (page 111) that you should always cross line. That goes for ceilings just as much as walls. Therefore, your ceiling lining paper should go at right angles to the window wall – ie in the opposite direction to that recommended for the ceiling paper. In all other respects deal with it as I have already described.

Postscript

So there you are. You have finished the room. I hope you have made a good job of it . . . certainly, armed with the information in this book there is no reason why you should not have done so. But don't be in too much of a hurry to put the room back in commission again. When moving furniture back in, putting up the curtains, pictures and light fittings again, and especially when re-laying the floor covering, you will raise a fair amount of dust. Far better to ensure that everything has dried off, particularly the paint, before you do that.

In the meantime, there is your equipment to be stored away, and that is something to do properly, so that it will be in tip-top condition when you come to work again. Place the lids firmly on any half-empty paint tins and put them where you will be able to find them easily – you never know when you will want to use the paint left in them for touching up any damage to your new paint-work. For the same reason keep a little spare wallpaper in case any patching up is necessary. Clean your brushes thoroughly, and store them away carefully wrapped up. Put all your other equipment away safely, too. This is one of the most important tricks of the trade: buy good equipment and look after it . . . and in return it will look after you.

Index

Aluminium
  preparation 33
  priming 52
Anaglypta 76
  stripping 20

Blowlamps 22–5
Brushes
  paint 37–44
    cleaning 71–2
  paperhanging 82–3
  pasting 81
  wall and ceiling 38–41
Burning off 19, 23–5

Ceiling and wall brushes
  38–41
Ceilings
  painting 64–6, 70
  papering 113–18
  repairing 118–19
Chemical paint strippers
  25–6
Cleaning rollers and brushes
  70–2
Clearing the room 13–14
Concrete, papering 79
Copper, painting 33, 52
Corners
  wallpapering 95, 97–9
  hanging vinyls 107–8
Cracks, filling 27–32
Cross brushing 59–60
Cross lining 111–13

Cutting in 62–4
Cutting to length 89–90

Distempered surfaces,
  papering 78
Door jamb dusters 43
Doors, painting 58–9, 61–2
Doorways, wallpapering
  round 100–2
Dust, precautions against 14,
  57, 121

Eggshell paints 35–6
Emulsion-painted surfaces,
  papering 78
Emulsion paints 36–7
  applying 49–50, 64–7
  stripping 25
Equipment, care of 70–2, 121

Floors, coverings 14, 121
Filling 27–32
Filling knives 28–9
Fireplaces, papering round
  102
Flat varnish brushes 41–3
Flock papers 77
Floors, coverings 14, 121
Foils 77
Furniture
  clearing 13–14
  replacing 121

Gel gloss paints 35, 47, 56, 60
Gloss emulsion paints 36

Gloss-painted surfaces, papering 78
Gloss paints 35, 37
    applying 57–60

Hanging
    ceiling papers 114–18
        first length 114–17
    wallcoverings 93–113
        first drop 94–6
        last drop 97
    lining papers 110–13
    ready-pasteds 108–10
    vinyls 106–8
Hawk 28
Hessian 76–7
Holes, filling 27–32

Kettles, paint 53–4
Knives
    putty 29
    wallpapering 81
Knotting 45–6

Laying off 59–60
Light switches 99–101
Light roses, ceilings 118
Lining papers 110–13, 118–19
Liquid gloss paints 35, 57–60

Masking tape 14, 63
Measuring up 88
Metallic papers 77
Metalwork
    painting 47–8
    preparation 32–3
    priming 51–2
Mould removal 22

Non-drip paints 35, 47, 56, 60

Novamura 77

Oil paints 35–6

Paint brushes 37–44
Paint kettles 53–4
Paint rollers 68–70
Paint spats 18
Paint tins, opening 52–3
Painted papers, stripping 20
Painting on paint 47
Painting sequence 45
Paints and painting 34–72
    stripping 22–6
Paintwork, rubbing down 26–7
Papers, Papering see Wallcoverings, Wallpapering, Wallpapers
Paste
    mixing 87
    selecting 86
Pasting 90–3
Pasting tables 81–2
    calibrating 88
Patterns 90
    stairwells 106
Plaster, painting 48–50
Plumblines 93–4, 98, 103–4
Polystyrene wall linings 79
Preparation, 12–33, 77–9
Primers 46, 50–2
    applying 61
Putty knives 29

Ready-pasteds, hanging 108–10
Relief decorations 75–6
Reveals 103–5
Rollers, painting 68–70

Rubbing down paint 26–7
    between coats 48
Rule and pencil 80–1
Rust 32–3

Scaffold boards 15–16, 65–7,
    82, 111–12, 114, 117
Scissors, wallpapering 81
Scraping tools 17–19
Seam rollers 83,96
Shading wallpapers 89
Shave hooks 18–19
Silk finish paints 37
Sizing 89
Soaking ready-pasteds
    108–10
Soffits 103–5
Stairwells, papering 106
    scaffolding 16
Straining paint 55–6
Stripping paint 22–6
    wallpaper 19–22
Stripping powders 19
Supaglypta 76
    stripping 20

Thixotropic gloss paints 35,
    47, 56, 60
Toxic paints 56–7
Trimming wallcoverings
    doorways 100–2
    fireplaces 102
    light switches 99–100
    roses 118
    top and bottom 95
    vinyls 107–8

Undercoats 46–7
    applying 61

Vinaglypta 76

Vinyls 75
    hanging 106–8
    stripping 20–1

Wall and ceiling brushes
    38–41
Wallboards, papering 78–9
Wallcoverings
    choosing 74–7, 106
    quantities, estimating
    79–80
    shading rolls 89
Wallpapering 73–119
    apron 83
    cutting to length 89–90
    hanging 93–113
    measuring up 88
    order of work 83–6
    pasting 90–3
    sizing 89
    stripping 19–22
    surface preparation 77–9
    tools 80–3
    waste 106
Wallpapers 74–5
    washable 75
Walls, painting 66–7
Washable papers 75
    stripping 20–1
Washing down 21–2
Wet-and-dry 27
Whitewash, removal 26
Window frames
    burning off 19, 24–5
    painting 63–4
Window walls, papering
    102–6
Wood chip papers 76
Woodwork
    painting 45–7
    priming 51